Speaking that Connects

Present With Confidence and Engage Your Audience

By Eileen N. Sinett

Open Door Publications^{SM}, LLC

Speaking That Connects

Copyright © 2011 by Eileen N. Sinett

All names and identifying details of persons mentioned as examples in this book have been changed to protect the privacy of individuals.

All rights reserved.
Printed in the United States

No part of this book may be used or reproduced in any manner whatsoever without the written permission of the author except in the case of brief quotations embodied in critical articles and reviews.

Published by
Open Door Publications^{SM}, LLC
27 Carla Way
Lawrenceville, NJ 08648
www.OpenDoorPublications.com

ISBN: 9780982891889

This book is dedicated to everyone who has ever been afraid to be themselves.

Foreword

Speaking that Connects simplifies a process for developing and delivering successful presentations that satisfy you and your audience. The process involves three phases: thinking, doing and being. It is for novice, intermediate and seasoned speakers alike, who want to learn the *best* presentation practices and enjoy their speaking experience as they take center stage and engage with their audience.

Speaker satisfaction goes beyond well planned and packaged ideas. It is achieved when presenters risk sharing who they truly are and integrate thought and delivery with their own brand of personal presence. With this risk and integration, audience satisfaction is all but guaranteed!

While writing this book, a few well-meaning colleagues challenged me with two very important questions: *"What makes your book so different?"* and *"Why would anyone read yet another book on presentations?"* My answers surfaced surprisingly fast.

"Because this one is written by me, reflects my unique training, perspective, personality and spirit, and more than thirty years of experience working with speech development, speech differences, and speech-makers. Maybe the reader is still searching for something – information, validation or the feeling of being understood, and has not yet been satisfied with what he has read."

"Then again, maybe the reader just resonates or connects with the title, cover, layout or author's point of view. That's all it takes – some kind of connection!" Connection is key.

All Speech Coaches are NOT the Same

Speech coaches come from many walks of life that color their beliefs and how they work. There are speech coaches with backgrounds in broadcasting and media communications; speech coaches trained as actors and acting coaches; and speech coaches with expertise in organizational psychology, business management and marketing. There are also speechwriters, event planners, and training and development instructors who share the role of speech and presentation coach.

Though their goals are the same – to support public speaking confidence and drive presentation excellence – their strategies, viewed from their personal experience, expertise and emphasis, differ. I'm no exception.

My coaching style is a blend of several overlapping disciplines and I'd like to acknowledge the experiences that most influenced my speech coaching career. First and foremost, I recognize Emerson College, in Boston, Massachusetts, my undergraduate alma mater. Known for its specialization in the speech arts and communication sciences, Emerson groomed me as a speech professional. Course requirements in voice and articulation, dialects, debate and oral interpretation developed my ability to listen, speak without a New Jersey accent (most of the time) and value cadence, tone and language as I never had before.

Speech pathology courses taught me to think like a scientist. My ability to see expanded exponentially as I observed behaviors behind one-way mirrors. Helping speakers with physical challenges increased my capacity for compassion, intimacy and trust and developing personal improvement plans to assist different learning styles catapulted my creativity.

As a mental health clinician at the University of Medicine and Dentistry of New Jersey, I applied my technical speech-communication skills to individuals with emotional challenges to improve their relationships, self-expression and self-esteem. When my position was downsized, I decided to hang a shingle and became self-employed.

Private practice became my introduction to business. Now, I was buying my first business suit to work with a career management firm and studying strategic planning, accounting, advertising and marketing. "Patients" became clients who were professionals, small business owners and mid- to large-sized corporations.

Three decades later, it is evident that entrepreneurship agrees with me. I am responsible to myself, committed to my clients and constantly involved with new opportunities. Speech and communication remain my competencies, diversity and personal growth my interests, and helping people achieve presentation confidence and clarity, my passion. What I said as a professional first entering the workforce remains true today:

"As long as there are people, there will be work for me to do, since people are hardwired to speak and communicate to form relationships, and relationships are influenced by how people speak and communicate".

I suspect this will always be the case.

Table of Contents

Introduction 2

PART I: The THINKING STAGE
1. Massage Your Mind 9
2. Why You and Audience Who? 17
3. The Objective/Conclusion Coin 24
4. Getting Clear 29
5. Organize, Don't Memorize 33
6. Fleshing Out and Filling In 45
7. Openings that Connect 52
8. Visual Aids: Stimulate or Complicate 58
9. Transitions: Content Linkage 63
10. Q&A: Anticipate and Abbreviate 67

PART 2: The DOING STAGE
11. Self-Control and Other Control 73
12. Stand Still and Hold Your Ground 77
13. Eye Contact and Connection 80
14. Smile: A Non-verbal Social Lubricant 86
15. Voice: Lullaby, Dirge or Infomercial? 87
16. Absolutely Say *Yes* to Gestures 95
17. Q&A: When Monologue Becomes Dialogue 99
18. Coordinating Visual Aids With Speaking 103

PART 3: The BEING STAGE
19. Being: Connection to Self 117

PART 4: EXTERNALS, ENERGY AND OTHER CONSIDERATIONS

20. Environment, Event, Equipment.................. 129
21. Rehearsal and Practice............................ 140
22. Final Remarks 142

Acknowledgements 143

Appendix 145

SPEAKING THAT CONNECTS

Did you ever try out a new restaurant, totally enjoy the meal and not be able to stop telling all your friends how good it was?

Have you ever had a partner who understood what you liked and made you feel heavenly?

And, did you ever listen to a professor, speaker or favorite performing artist who left you feeling excited and wanting more?

In each of these scenarios the focus is on the recipients: of the meal, the intimacy, the performance or presentation. But, what about the "givers," the chef, the partner, the presenter, the performer? How did they feel?

Pleasing your audience is important, but the true measure of speaking success is when listeners **and** speakers feel satisfied. Speaking that Connects shows you how to achieve both.

INTRODUCTION

With caring yet critical eyes and ears, I watched as professionals delivered their "baseline" presentations as part of a corporate training I was facilitating. While most demonstrated the usual array of pre-training nervous mannerisms, delivery faux pas and content overload, one speaker absolutely wowed me.

"Are you a ringer?" I asked the participant. Mark looked embarrassed and puzzled.

"Are you here to check up on me, to see if I know what I'm doing as a trainer?" Again he wore an expression of shock.

"That was a phenomenal presentation! I'm not sure I can teach you anything more. Your message was well crafted and your delivery was engaging, professional and polished. You were great! You do realize how well you present, don't you?"

Mark started to visibly fidget, fingers curled and wiggling against his palms. "That really wasn't me," he muttered.

"Well if you're not a ringer, and that wasn't you, then, are you a phony?" I asked.

I don't know what possessed me to confront Mark with those specific words. I suppose my intuition must have been on automatic pilot. That question zapped Mark's emotional equilibrium and was later acknowledged as the transformational moment that catapulted his personal growth. A month after the training, Mark confessed his secret, that without his anxiety medication, he would never have gotten through the dozens of career presentations that won him promotions and his current executive status. Perceiving his performance as medication-dependent, Mark felt his success to be outside himself. With this belief, he was unable to allow his true self to be present and to enjoy what his audience so appreciated.

Mark's story underscores the fact that **what an audience sees and hears is not the whole picture.** Mark could fool his audience, but not himself. Physically, he was in the room, polished and intelligent, but emotionally and spiritually, Mark was somewhere else. Although Mark satisfied his listeners, he could not achieve his own speaking satisfaction.

As a result of this confrontation, Mark embarked on a self-awareness journey, and I learned even more deeply how intrinsically important *the inside* is to the *whole*. A presenter may execute a strong performance yet not feel connected to himself, his material or his listeners. To the audience, the performance is effective and satisfying. But this is insufficient. From my perspective as a speech coach, **the true measure of speaking success is when both speaker and audience feel mutually satisfied.**

The Number One Fear on the Book of Lists

Public speaking is the number one fear on *The Book of Lists*,[1] and I suspect it will remain there until our education system changes. Well-meaning teachers need to realize the impact of asking our children to speak in front of a class without first providing them with any training or general guidance. To assume that because most children can speak to friends or family with ease, they "should" be equally comfortable speaking to a group, is a false assumption and one that can bear long-term scars. I know this to be true, because some of these children grow up to be my clients: executives, professionals and entrepreneurs.

Talking to a group is energetically different than talking to one person at a time, just as standing and talking to a group is different than sitting and talking to the same group. I can't count how many times clients have said, "I speak fine "one-to-one" or "I can present if I'm sitting down."

When environment, expectations and energy are unfamiliar, people are often uncomfortable. They feel unnatural and thrown off course and their body reacts. We know this as nervousness. It's not so much the number of people in the room, but the concentrated **energy** of the listeners focused on the speaker that causes this discomfort. Let's face it. Speaking to groups occurs much less frequently than speaking in conversations or discussions. For these, you neither have the responsibility of doing all the talking, nor do you need to stand. New experiences without guidance or practice are a prescription for nervousness. The antidote is knowledge and rehearsal.

---

[1] Wallechinsky, David and Wallace, Amy, **The People's Almanac's The Book of Lists,** William Morrow and Company, Inc., New York, 1977, p.469.
The Gallop Poll Survey of 2001 indicated that public speaking ranked second, with fear of snakes being the number one fear.

Many clients have shared their shame, embarrassment and terror of delivering that first school book report or show-and-tell speech. Some realize their center-stage pain often relates to feeling different because of how they look: too tall, too black, too fat or ethnic. Others' complaints relate to feeling awkward and uncomfortable before a group because of innate shyness, insecurity about their knowledge or their right to express themselves. And there have been clients whose public speaking fears are linked to having been the new kid on the block, to the need to be perfect, to having been criticized by an authority or to the fear of letting people down.

I have a twenty-year-old daughter. When she was in the third grade she was required to do an oral presentation, not a book report or show-and-tell. Her teachers explained the expectations upon which she would be graded: posture, passion for her subject, organization of ideas, gestures, even how to answer difficult questions without being defensive.

Moreover, these skills were modeled and taught so the students were more likely to succeed. I often wonder if all students were given these tools *before* they navigated these unchartered public speaking waters, would we produce more confident adult speakers? Would public speaking lose its place at the top of the list of fears in the Book of Lists? I definitely think so.

Nature or Nurture?

I believe that anyone can be a public speaker and a decent one at that – if they want to be, are true to themselves and are willing to learn and practice a few skills. *Speaking that Connects* is a **process** that develops presentation clarity, speaker confidence and audience connection. Typical of processes, its goals are to streamline effort, enhance efficiency and increase productivity and success. The three phases in the Speaking that Connects process are: Thinking, Doing and Being.

Whether you are a novice, intermediate or seasoned speaker, I hope you will embrace the simplicity of this model and integrate these techniques into your speaking repertoire. They are intended to enhance your personal and professional growth, raise the bar on presentation performance and promote speaker and audience satisfaction.

Let's begin.

PART I
THE THINKING STAGE

"Sometimes only a change of viewpoint is needed to convert a tiresome duty into an interesting opportunity."
Alberta Flanders

"Fear is born in uncertainty and nourished by pessimism"
Lois Wyse

Chapter 1
Massage Your Mind

There are ten thinking steps in this first phase of the Speaking that Connects process, but there is no need to panic. Many of these tasks require simple self-reflection and are not at all time-consuming. Think of these steps as three sets of three plus one and they become much more easily managed.

Step 1: Manage your Mindset

You are told that you will have a public speaking role, or you may want a speaking opportunity to grow your business or career. In either case, if your first reaction is *"Oh no," "Nobody's going to listen to me"* or *"I'd rather die than make a speech,"* you've got some mindset management work to do. Before you start preparing your content, you will need to adjust your attitude.

Satisfaction begins with thought and thoughts drive reality. As in the game *Monopoly*, you cannot pass *Go* (plan your presentation message) and collect the reward (feel satisfied with your speaking performance) until you let yourself out of jail (eliminate or neutralize negative thinking).

Despite an infinite number of possible responses, people react automatically with comments based upon their conditioned belief systems. These often negative, knee-jerk reactions are like self-imposed sentences that limit one's potential. Conscious or unconscious compromising thoughts are often the cause of presentation anxiety. If you want to give yourself a fair shake at public speaking success, practice transforming your negative thoughts into more positive or neutral ones.

For example, to the request, *"I'd like you to be our speaker at the meeting,"* your automatic response might be:

- *No, not me*
- *I can't*
- *This isn't my forte*
- *I'm going to bomb*
- *I'll have a heart attack*
- *I have to find someone else, etc.*

However, you can have these thoughts and simultaneously choose to say different words and still remain true to yourself. So to the request, *"I'd like you to be our speaker at the meeting,"* you can also say:

- *OK*
- *I'll do my best*
- *I may need some help*
- *This could be a good opportunity*
- *I would like to succeed*
- *I can do this*

Language is infinite; we need to become comfortable with exercising our linguistic options.

Exercise: Reframing Negatives

Reframing negative statements into neutral or positive ones alters self-imposed limitations. Without these barriers, you create the space for other thoughts and behaviors to exist. Although managing your negative thoughts may feel unfamiliar or awkward at first, with a little practice you can silence the critic, lessen the fear and give voice to more positive wants.

Below are examples of automatic negative responses and two reframed alternatives.

A. *I always blank out and make a fool of myself.*
   1. I want to manage my fear of blanking out.
   2. I want to move through this fear.

B. *I'm lousy at this.*
   1. I want to do well.
   2. I have valuable information to share.

C. *People will laugh at me.*
   1. I want people to smile with me.
   2. I want people to enjoy what I have to say.

Notice that automatic negative responses tend to be comments that are absolute (always/never), self-judging (I'm lousy) or statements focused on the future, (People will laugh). Also note that the reframed negatives are **statements of what you want.**

What do **you** say to yourself when asked to make a presentation? Are your thoughts positive, negative or neutral? Fact or fiction? Focused on the present, past or future? If your tendency is to self-deprecate, project doom or gloom, or give yourself a hard time, you may need to give yourself a kinder mental massage.

Exercise:

Write what your inner voice says when you hear, *"We'd like you to present (at our next meeting, to the Board, on stage, before a thousand people, at church, etc)."* Then write two positive or neutral statements that could also be true.

Negative Response 1

_____

Reframed Response

1. _____
2. _____

Negative Response 2

_____

Reframed Response

1. _____
2. _____

This exercise is not about denying any negative feelings. *I am fearful* is not a negative, but a fact. *I feel unworthy, scared, awkward, unintelligent,* etc., can be your truth. Your feelings are your feelings. They need to be acknowledged and respected.

But uncomfortable feelings can coexist with other neutral or positive statements. *I am fearful and I want comfort; I feel stupid and I crave intelligence; I feel ugly and I desire beauty.*

Listen to the language of your thoughts and commit to neutralizing negatives. Allowing feelings of fear to coexist with more positive communication is the starting point to the Thinking portion of the Speaking that Connects process.

Why Two Alternatives?

That's a great question, and here's the answer: **The first positive or neutral response balances or cancels out the negative, while the second positive or neutral response reinforces the positive and moves you forward.**

Consider each negative comment you make as money you debit from your public speaking bank account. When you say something negative about your speaking ability or future performance, you are making a withdrawal from the account. If you then add a positive statement, you make a deposit that brings your balance to where it originally was before that debit or withdrawal. **To build your speaking confidence and move your comfort level forward, you need to make more positive deposits.** The following chart illustrates this point.

Figure 1.1

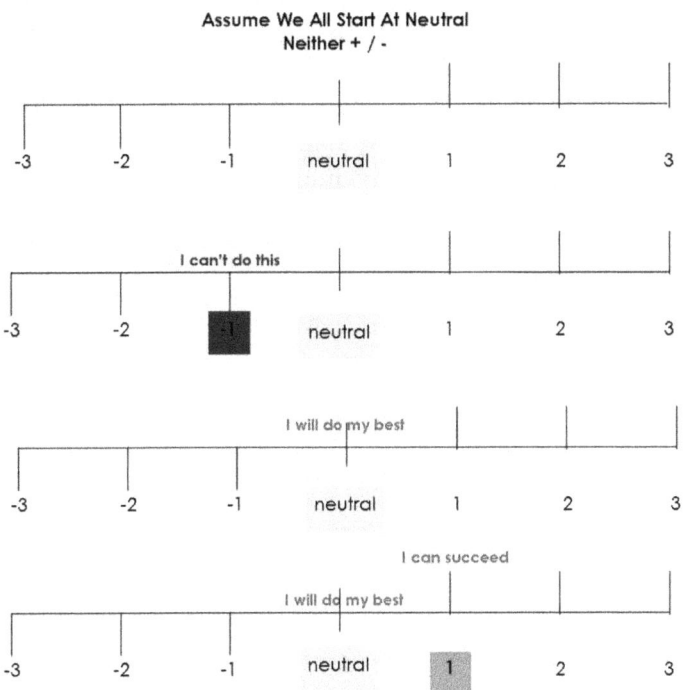

Over the years, many people, myself included, have operated from a half-empty versus half-full frame of reference. Family, educators and religious teachings have often been unintentionally at fault. As a result, many productive and successful people blatantly or secretly harbor self-doubt and low self-esteem because they have bought into our parental, educational, and religious *half-empty* conditioning.

I don't believe for a second that as infants we thought of ourselves in this *"less than"* way. We were once free, and that was "BS": before school, before social conformity, before being shaped into what others wanted us to be. We need to get back to zero, to this beginning place where we are naturally open and non-judgmental.

Rephrasing negatives into neutrals or positives is freeing. It creates a shift in perspective and opens the door to new realities. Over time, this practice can transform your cup from half-empty to half-full, so that half-full becomes your new, automatic response.

In the words of my mother and perhaps yours as well, *"If you can't say anything nice about somebody, don't say anything at all."* I agree. And guess what? You are one of those somebodies. So make managing your mindset your first and foremost presentation thinking to-do!

THINKING REVIEW

✓ Step 1: Manage Your Mindset

Chapter 2
Why YOU and Audience WHO?

Step 2: Analyze your Audience; Know Why You are Speaking

You may be thinking that once the matter of mindset has been managed, it is time to focus on your presentation message. However, don't be in too much of a hurry. There's still some presentation foreplay required that will ultimately support your presentation performance!

It is smart, logical and necessary to spend some time reflecting on questions relating to you as a speaker and to the audience who will be listening to you. This is your Thinking Step 2.

Actually, when it comes to thinking about your audience, you automatically think about yourself. You rarely have one without the other. If either the speaker or audience is absent, there may be speech, but no communication. The nature of presentations is the dynamic between speaker and audience. Creating a speech without considering your audience is like preparing a vegetarian gourmet meal for a hardcore carnivore or giving your partner a loving backrub when she really wants a passionate kiss.

Let's begin with questions about you. You have been asked to speak for a reason. **What makes you credible to speak to this audience?**

Write out your answers to anchor the information deeply into your cells, or if you prefer, answer the questions aloud. Voicing your responses and writing them down both transform thought into action.

Exercise: Questions about You, the Speaker
Reflect on these questions. Then write your responses.

What is my area of expertise?

_____

Why am I speaking to this particular group?

_____

_____

_____

Was I selected, or did I seek this opportunity?

_____

What is my relationship to the topic, to the audience, to the event?

_____

_____

_____

As a result of speaking, what outcomes are possible?

_____

_____

_____

Once you get clear on the *why you,* ask strategic questions about your audience. Though you may not know everyone who will be attending your presentation, reflecting on what you do know about your audience is integral to your presentation preparation.

Exercise: Questions about Your Audience

Reflect on these questions. Then write your responses below relative to a particular presentation you plan to present.

Who is my audience?

_____

_____

What do I know about them? Age, Gender, Race, Professional level, Disciplines

_____

_____

Why are they coming to the presentation?

_____

_____

What do they need to know and why?

_____

_____

How many people are expected?

_____

In what ways am I similar to this audience? (What do I have/know/like in common with the audience?)

_____

_____

In what ways are we different?

_____

_____

_____

Who am I threatened by and why?

_____

_____

_____

Your Own Listening Preferences

Besides understanding your specific audience, why and how they listen, you will benefit from thinking about your own experience when you are part of an audience. Consider what makes **you** listen to a presenter. What holds **your** attention? What works for **you?**

These are some things that keep listeners listening:

- New information
- Information that can be applied immediately
- Logical organization of information
- Not too much detail
- A clear message
- Understanding how this information affects me
- Enthusiasm and passion
- Credibility and name recognition
- Interesting storyline
- A creative opening
- Humor
- Confidence and charisma
- Interesting PowerPoint slides
- Good handouts
- A speaker who cares
- An attractive speaking voice

Some people like information they can use. Others require enthusiasm to make them pay attention. Some stop listening if they don't like the speaker's hairstyle, and others will listen to the speaker's every word with the intent of finding fault.

Thinking about what satisfies you as a listener will help you satisfy your audience.

THINKING REVIEW

- ✓ Step 1: Manage Your Mindset
- ✓ Step 2: Answer Why YOU and Audience WHO

Chapter 3
The Objective/Conclusion Coin

Step 3: Turn Your Objective into a Conclusion

Your objective and conclusion are like long-term lovers. They complement each other and are intimately related.

Like two sides of a coin, they exist as one. Your objective is what you, the speaker wants, and is focused on the future outcome. The conclusion is what you want the audience to receive. It is focused on the action that you want them to take.

Here are some objective-conclusion examples to get you started.

Example A
Objective:
To persuade colleagues to accept a change
Conclusion:
This change will lighten the workload and give us all the extra time we need to do what we do best.

Example B
Objective:
To convince upper management of the need for additional resources
Conclusion:
With the understanding of the scope of the project and the leadership behind it, we hope you will approve these resources so we can launch by the end of first quarter.

Example C
Objective:
   To sell a newly-released book
Conclusion:
   Speaking that Connects is a simple, friendly and professional process that gives you the tools you need to succeed as a presenter. It's a resource you'll want on your bookshelf.

Example D
Objective:
   To inform management on current expenditures compared to budget and obtain their confidence
Conclusion:
   This summarizes our current expenditures relative to our budget. We project to be on target.

Now, why are **you** presenting? What is **your** purpose? What do **you** want to happen as a result of your presentation?

To help you refine your focus and efficiently time-manage your presentation planning, answer one or all of the following questions:

Exercise: Objective/Conclusion

At the end of my presentation, I want the audience to:

_____

_____

The most important message I want the group to remember is:

_____

_____

_____

What's important about my message is:

_____

_____

_____

_____

Write your presentation objective and rework it as your conclusion.

My objective is:

_____

_____

_____

_____

_____

My conclusion is:

_____

_____

_____

Remember: the conclusion is the key message and core of your presentation. It's your audience's takeaway. Be clear about your objective and translate it into a conclusion.

THINKING REVIEW

- ✓ Step 1: Manage Your Mindset
- ✓ Step 2: Answer Why YOU and Audience WHO
- ✓ Step 3: Turn Your Objective into a Conclusion

Chapter 4
Getting Clear

Step 4: Brainstorm on Paper

Sometimes you get stuck. You might not clearly know your topic, objective or conclusion and consequently have trouble planning your presentation. As with taking a vacation or a romantic getaway, you might know that you want to relax and be in the sun (objective) but not know your direction or destination (Miami? Jamaica? Aruba?)

Many of my clients stress out at this initial stage of planning, often spending too much time going nowhere.

Let's look at this example. A marketing entrepreneur is asked to speak at a Chamber of Commerce dinner. The audience is comprised of diverse business professionals, and the speaker has a plethora of potential topics he could speak on, but doesn't know where to begin.

To get clear on the focus of his presentation, he used this two-minute, mind-mapping exercise that I call a "brainstorming on paper." Figure 4.1 shows the marketing professional's mind map. This is how this exercise works.

To brainstorm on paper, you use the sunburst graphic indicated in figure 4.2. **Print "TOPIC"** in the center of the circle and ask yourself: *What could I talk about to this group?* **Set a timer for two minutes** and on each *sunray* write the ideas that spontaneously pop into your mind.

Write quickly without screening or mentally editing your thoughts. Simply write your ideas onto the rays. Cursive or print, upper or lowercase and shorthand are all fine.

Usually, three or more ideas emerge within the first fifteen seconds. Then, there might be a lull. That's fine. Let there be a lull! Ask again, *what am I able to talk about?* More ideas usually emerge.

When your two minutes are up, finish writing your last thought and STOP! You now have a selection of topics from which to choose the subject of your presentation.

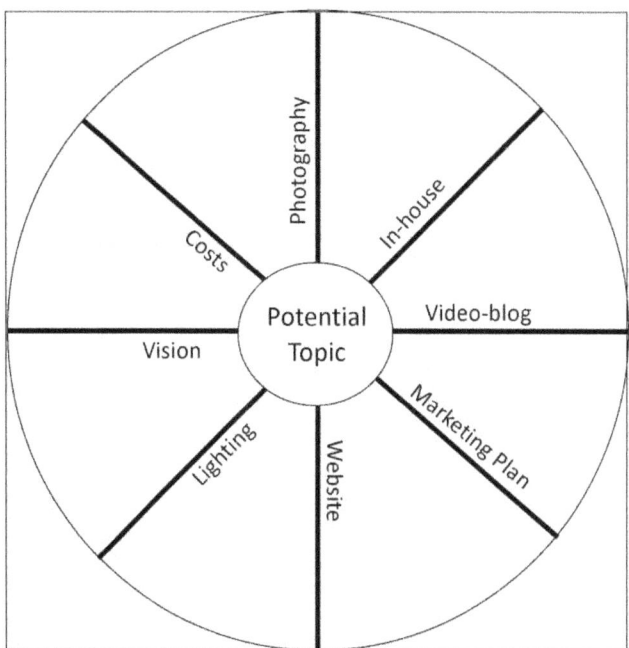

Figure 4.1 Brainstorming on Paper

This method is short and sweet and works! You limit the time you spend "inside your head" thinking, and transform the internal energy of thought into the external energy of written communication. With your topic now identified, you are free to move forward.

This tool can be used whenever you feel stumped.

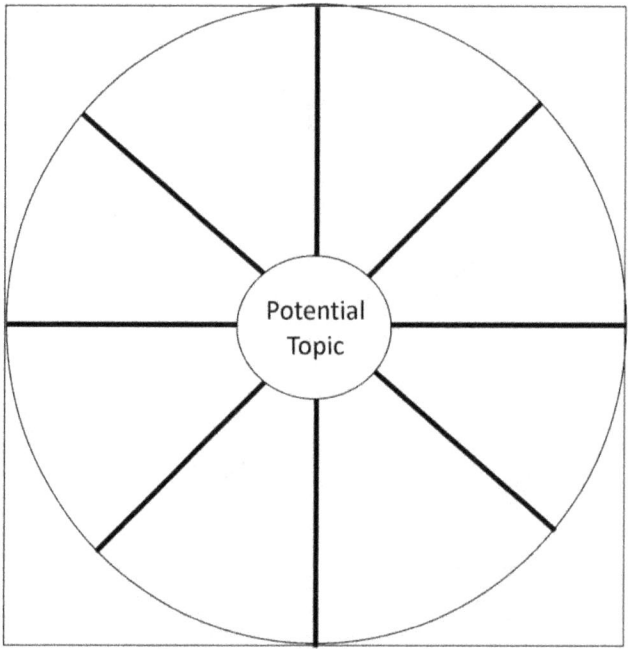

Figure 4.2 Brainstorming on Paper

Simply write a need in the center of the starburst and ask a question of possibility. Then let your ideas emerge naturally. This exercise can be for used many types of situations where there is an impasse. For example, one client brainstorms on paper to plan his report-writing; another uses this tool to prioritize her daily tasks.

THINKING REVIEW

- ✓ Step 1: Manage Your Mindset
- ✓ Step 2: Answer Why YOU and Audience WHO
- ✓ Step 3: Turn Your Objective into a Conclusion
- ✓ Step 4: Brainstorm on Paper

Chapter 5
Organize, Don't Memorize

Thinking Step 5: Organize and Format your "Flow"

Too many intelligent professionals start their presentation planning by cutting and pasting slides from previous talks or by writing their speeches out word-for-word, manuscript style. Though the manuscript method works for some, it does not work for most. It generally leads to lengthy rewrites, increased anxiety and wasted time. The only exception is your opening which we'll talk about in Chapter 7.

There are two main reasons why writing your speech out word for word is unadvisable. First, a written speech sets the speaker up for reading and/or memorization. This almost always results in memory lapses and a struggle to recall what the speaker remembers seeing written on the page. **The speaker's attention becomes split between his visual memory of the printed word which he created in the past and his ability to communicate ideas and connect with his audience in the present.** The consequences are often awkward apologies, compromised credibility, and disconnection from self, audience, and material.

I have painfully watched speakers, who, having committed their presentations to memory, forget a word, and then completely short-circuit, unable to speak at all. Like telemarketers who must read their telephone pitches from start to finish without customer interruption, presenters who rely upon memorization often fall short of presentation success. They never get to "own" their content. Even when speakers succeed in memorizing their perfectly written-out speeches, they often talk about feeling "in their heads" and dissociated from their inner selves.

Unconsciously they have prioritized the printed word over the listeners in the room.

The second reason for not reading or memorizing a speech has to do with the differences between spoken and written language. Written language is formal and intended for a reader. Spoken language is more casual and intended for a listener. Unless your speech is for a literary competition, presidential address, or similar form of formal oratory, it is best to speak in a conversational style to connect with your listeners. It makes perfect sense. If your audience is to learn by listening, then speak in a spoken style to keep them aurally-engaged.

One more very important point should be considered. When you write, you rarely see your audience read. When you speak, you almost always see your audience listen!

Get on with the 'Flow'

Sometimes presenters have so much information they have trouble organizing their speeches. They generally know their subject well, sometimes too well, and may not be able to see the forest through the trees. These speakers need help focusing and streamlining their messages. When you are an expert in an area, sometimes "everything" seems important. Many presenters, wanting to cover all their bases, tend to err on the side of "more is better." However, this is a mistake.

Too much information can dilute your message and dampen your audience's attention. The average adult listening attention span is just twenty minutes, even though our high school and college curricula are structured for forty-five minutes to two hours. Likewise, corporate presentations often tip the scale in the direction of "too much" and "too long," making audiences "too tired."

A speaker must remember that he is always competing with the audience's tendency to go away. The individuals in the audience may look like they are listening, but their minds might be "out to lunch," thinking about deadlines or half-finished work, getting to their kids' soccer game on time, or completing the last-minute plans of a much-needed getaway.

Because a presenter has a hundred percent of the speaking responsibility, the audience must listen for longer intervals than they are used to, as compared to more typical communications such as conversations and discussions.

Let's face it. Listening is an extremely complex mental activity requiring full attention, focus, understanding, and evaluation. It requires individuals to ignore external and internal distractions and stay present. And remember this: **While we were taught to read and write in elementary school, we did not receive very much if any, classroom instruction on how to listen or speak!**

Organizational Tools that Help

There are several ways people organize their presentations. Some use traditional outlines while others use more right-brain, mind-mapping skills. Some create ideas on Post-It notes and shuffle them around to create a "story," while others organize by writing in manuscript form.

Formats, or "flow-grams," also known as presentation templates, are great organizational planning tools that support time management and learning without memorization. They are simple to use and streamline the preparation process. Many clients report they will never return to writing out speeches word-for-word again. They are grateful for the simplicity that allows them to create and own their presentations in record time.

I have found that using organizational formats or templates significantly expedites the planning process. The schematic I use to develop my own and my clients' presentations can be seen in Figure 5.1. This flowchart reflects public speaking essentials that date back to Aristotle.

Sandwiched between an opening and a closing is the ***tell them what you will tell them*** (preview), ***tell them*** (content), and ***tell them what you told them*** (recap) organization. This format allows the presenter to map out his direction, see his full outline on one page and use conversational speech, rather than written language, to engage his audience.

Formats support a speaker's knowledge and memory and can be better organizational tools than the linear outlines studied in grade school. Formats support memory because of their landscape, view-at-a-glance design and the integration of right and left brain processing (shapes are generally processed by the right brain hemisphere, while words are processed by the left).

Let's move this presentation to the next level of organization by completing the format in figure 5.1. For now, skip the box at the top labeled "Opening." Openings are to your presentations what icing is to cake. They are added last, once the presentation is already "baked."

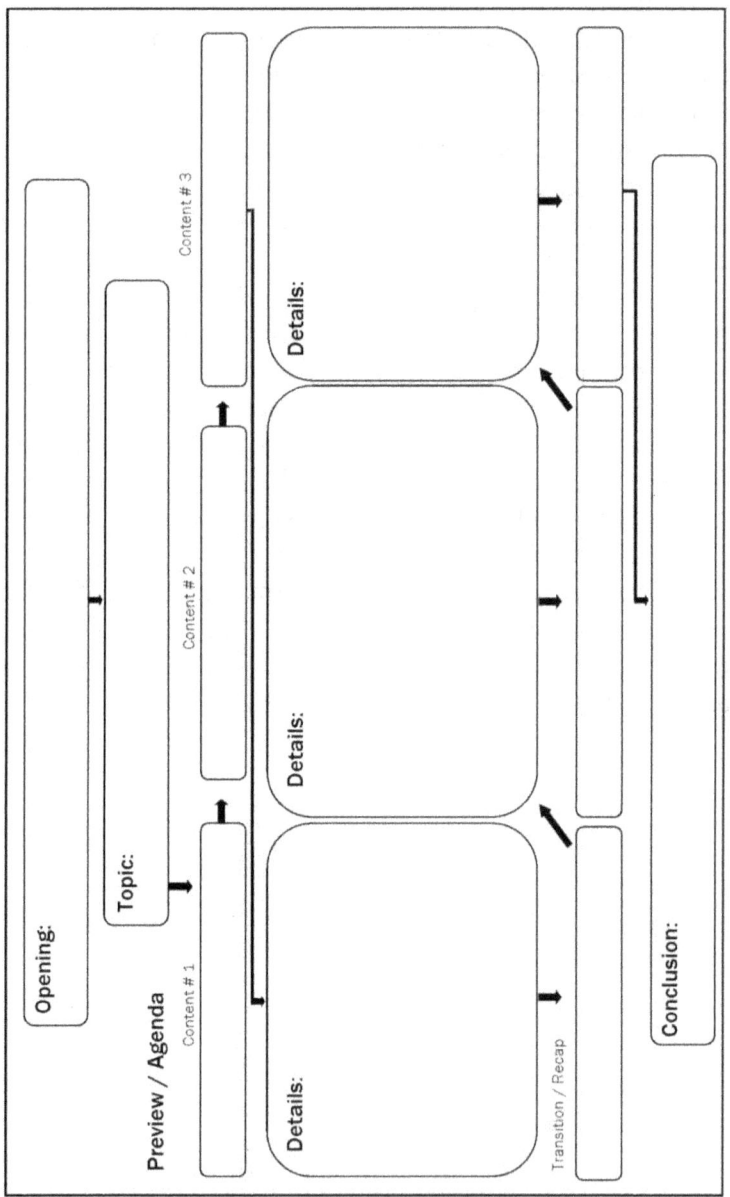

Figure 5.1 Format Worksheet

Filling out the Format

Using the template in Figure 5.1 **PRINT** your topic in **CAPITAL LETTERS** in the box marked "**TOPIC**." Printing in capital letters is important because it requires more concentration and more deliberate focus than writing in cursive or printing in upper and lower case letters. Print as neatly as you can, inhibiting the tendency to quickly move onto the next task. Printing supports learning your content flow and integrating it into your memory. **Be present and fully focused as you print!**

PRINT your Conclusion

After entering your topic, enter your conclusion, which you previously determined in Thinking Step 3. Then write your conclusion word-for-word. Remember, this is the statement you want your audience to remember long after your speech is over. Figure 5.2 shows these two steps for the topic, PRESENTATIONS.

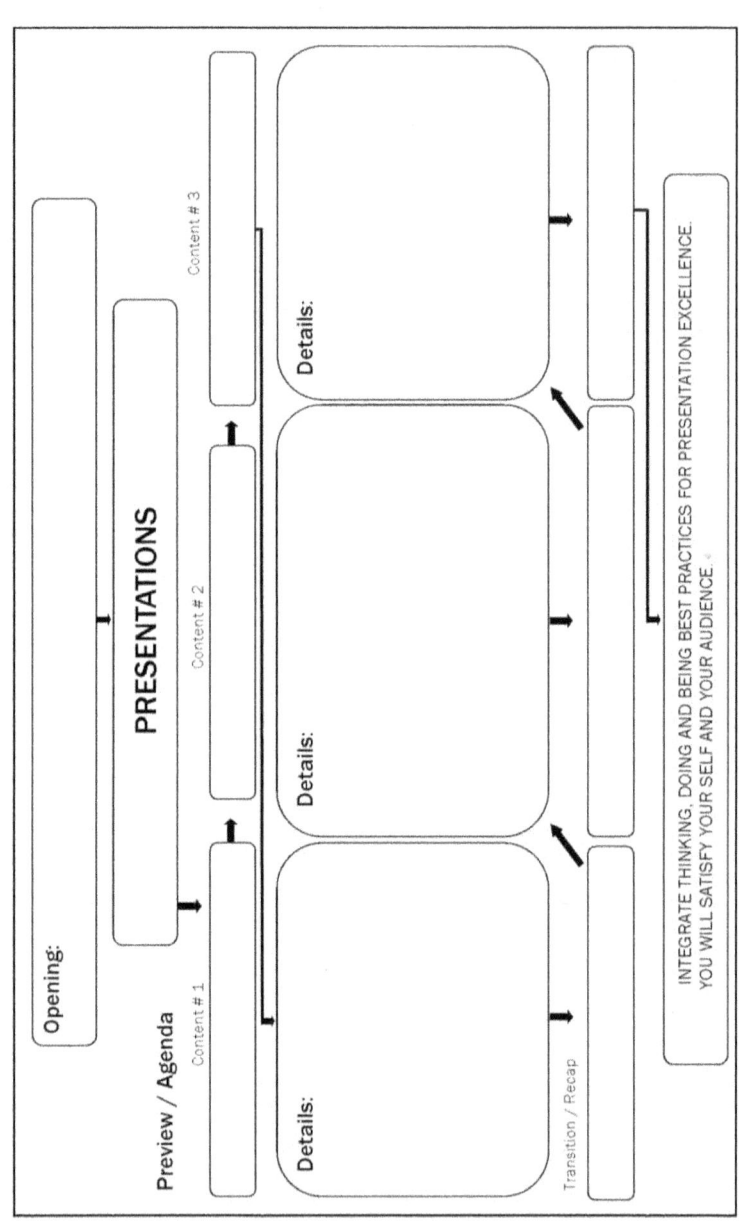

Figure 5.2 Format Worksheet

Content and Agenda

Moving to the Preview/Agenda area, identify three **categories** of information that support your topic and key message. These are your Content 1, Content 2, and Content 3 boxes. In Figure 5.3, I have completed these three steps for a presentation on PRESENTATIONS.

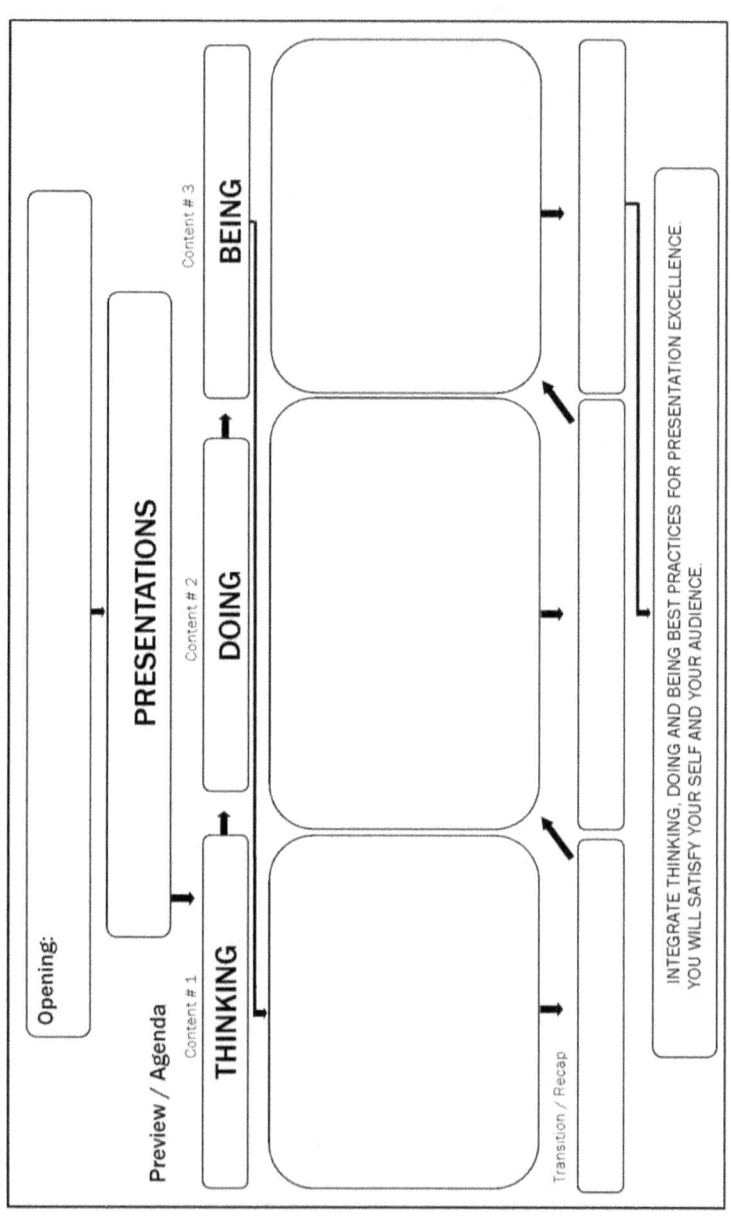

Figure 5.3 Format Worksheet

Okay, I can hear some readers questioning, "Why three?" and some others complaining that they have more than three areas of information to present. First, why three?

People respond positively to the number three. There's a universal rhythm and cadence that just *feels* right: red, white, and, blue; life, liberty, and the pursuit of happiness; vanilla, chocolate and strawberry; morning, noon, and night; breakfast, lunch, and dinner; beginning, middle, and end, thinking, doing and being. There seems to be an unconscious human preference for the rhythm of three that is by the way, also cross-cultural. In addition, adult learning research indicates that the average person remembers three to five ideas plus or minus two, or a total of one to seven ideas! **So, build your talk around three categories to support the memory recall of the majority!**

Now what to do when you have more than three content categories? Organize your information in chunks of three if at all possible. This will help your audience digest your presentation meal (appetizer, entrée, and dessert).

Returning to your format, decide on the three words that will be your presentation landmarks, direct your story and support your conclusion.

You can use the *Brainstorm on Paper* exercise in figure 4.1 to help you identify the three content areas for your speech. Again, set the timer for two minutes only. Print CONTENT in capital letters in your sunburst graphic and see what categories emerge. Discard any redundancies. Acknowledge what "feels right" and choose the three areas that will now become your presentation landmarks.

It is important to remember that these words represent categories. Think about going to the supermarket where there are sections for produce, dairy, meat, dry goods, etc. You are not going down an apple aisle or an egg aisle. You are in the fruit or dairy section. Similarly in a library or bookstore, you look for a specific title by first going to the appropriate book section such as: mysteries, sports, biographies, art, self-help, psychology, etc.

Here are some examples of categories that are often used for business presentations. Read these categories in groups of three, from left to right.

Content 1	Content 2	Content 3
Objectives	Strategy	Implementation
Project Design	Installation	Costs
Hypothesis	Results	Analysis
Background	Current Situation	Future Potential
Most Important	Next Important	Least Important
Plan	Assignments	Deadlines
Before	During	After
Observation	Analysis	Decision
Options	Comparison	Choice
Recap	Update	Forecast
Need	Solution	Benefits
Potential Benefits	Potential Negatives	Recommendations

Now using the Figure 5.1 form, **PRINT** these three words in the **Preview/Agenda** boxes, labeled **Content 1, 2, 3**. These words are your agenda, set your direction and help you stay on course, which helps your audience understand your logic and message and supports their listening attention.

Congratulations! At this stage you have the skeletal structure of your speech in place. With just this amount of preparation completed, you could easily give a 30-second commercial or even a two-minute overview of your twenty to forty-five minute talk.

THINKING REVIEW

- ✓ Step 1: Manage Your Mindset
- ✓ Step 2: Answer Why YOU and Audience WHO
- ✓ Step 3: Turn Your Objective into a Conclusion
- ✓ Step 4: Brainstorm on Paper to Get Clear
- ✓ Step 5: Organize Content in 3's

Chapter 6
Fleshing Out and Filling In

Step 6: Add Detail, Facts, and Anecdotes

Reviewing your work with the presentation template so far, you have identified the Topic, Conclusion, and three areas of Content, which become your Preview or Agenda. You have dug the foundation and built your presentation framework and are now ready to concentrate on your three specific "rooms," or your presentation interior. The following illustrates the process so far.

Example 1:
TOPIC: PRESENTATIONS

Audience: Professionals
Objective: To help professionals prepare and deliver presentations that audiences enjoy

CONCLUSION:
Thinking, doing, and being skills drive presentation excellence.

PREVIEW/AGENDA/CONTENT:
(1) THINKING (2) DOING (3) BEING

Content 1: THINKING
Detail 1
- Manage your mindset
- Utilize audience checklist
- List three reasons why you are speaking to this group
- Use formats to manage time efficiently

Content 2: DOING
Detail 2
- Stand still to start
- Breathe
- Speak louder than your conversational voice
- Allow gestures

Content 3: BEING
Detail 3
- Be in the present moment
- Hear your breath
- Stay present in your body

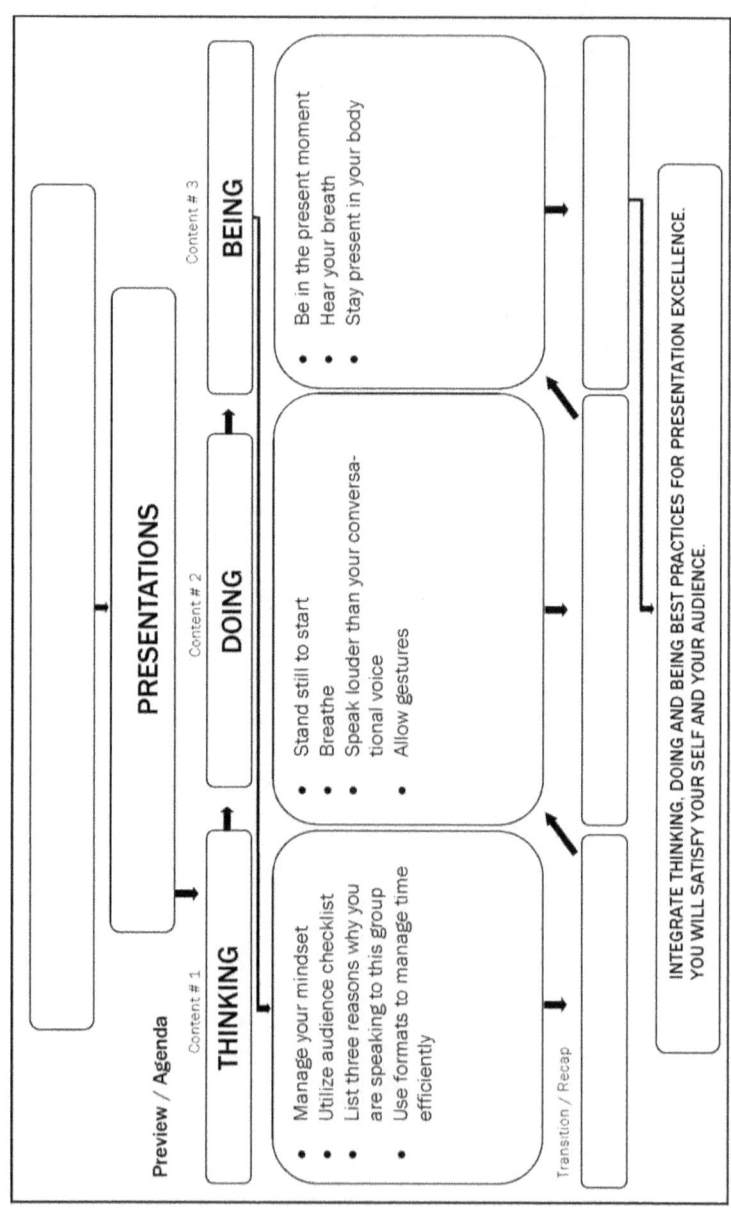

Figure 6.1 Format Worksheet

Here's another example for a different presentation.

TOPIC: PHOTOGRAPHY & VIDEO IN MARKETING

Audience: seasoned business owners
Objective: to heighten awareness of the value of video and photography and attract potential customers

CONCLUSION:
Knowing how to use photography and video for your business will give your brand a competitive advantage.

PREVIEW/AGENDA/CONTENT
(1) WHY (2) CONSIDERATIONS (3) HOW

Content 1: WHY
Detail 1
- Vision is consumer's key sense
- Pictures worth 1000 words
- Good visual input drives business

Content 2: CONSIDERATIONS
Detail 2
- Video or stills
- Black & white/color
- Composition
- Lighting

Content 3: HOW
Detail 3
- Home made
- Marketing middle man
- Professional videographer

Figure 6.2 shows the formatted organization of this topic.

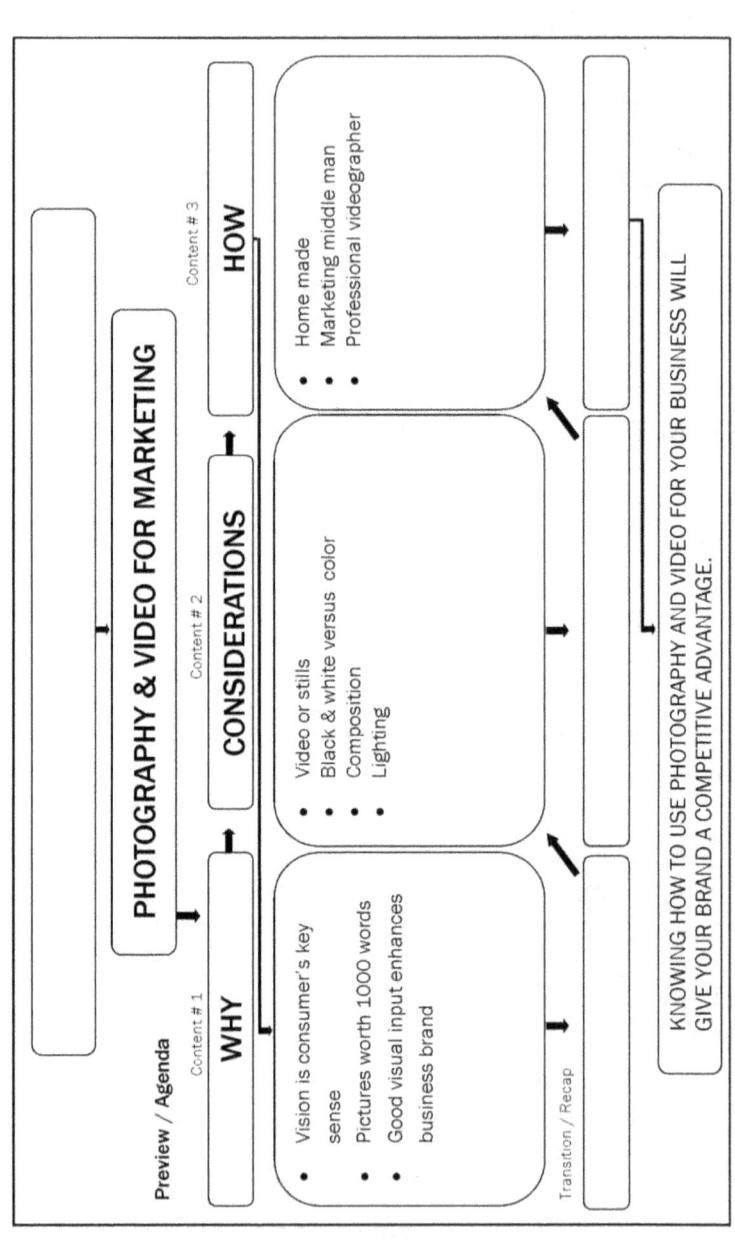

Figure 6.2 Format Worksheet

Return to Figure 5.1 on page 35 (or copy the form on page 149) and fill in the detail for your presentation topic. Limit your detail to no more than five sub-ideas per content area.

THINKING REVIEW

- ✓ Step 1: Manage Your Mindset
- ✓ Step 2: Answer Why YOU and Audience WHO
- ✓ Step 3: Turn Your Objective into a Conclusion
- ✓ Step 4: Brainstorm on Paper to Get Clear
- ✓ Step 5: Organize Content in 3's
- ✓ Step 6: Flesh Out and Fill In With Details

Chapter 7
Openings that Connect

Step 7: Create an Opening that Piques Listener Interest

Your opening is what people hear first and may determine whether your audience will continue to listen with an open mind, turn off completely, or judge you positively or negatively. While many, and maybe most in the audience have been conditioned to accept average as usual, know that **a strong start can give you a speaking advantage.**

Strong openings often translate to strong speaker. A memorable and creative opening will have your audience thinking of you as memorable and creative. Starting your presentation in a way that piques your audience's attention separates the pros from the novices.

So what is a good opening? Here are some possibilities.

- Personal stories or anecdotes (keep succinct)
- Startling facts (create disbelief or shock value)
- Rhetorical questions (get **your** question in **their** minds)
- Quotes (add credibility of others which gets attached to you)
- Assertive position statements (express strength of conviction)

On the next page are examples of openings used for a talk on presentations.

Anecdote
I complimented a speaker who I felt did a phenomenal presentation. You know what he said? *That wasn't me. I can't speak. I'll never be good at this.* This proves to me that speaking satisfaction is more than a standing ovation.

Glaring Fact
Public speaking is dreaded more than death or the dentist's drill!

Rhetorical Question
How many people here had a presentation course in the third grade?

Quote
Franklin D. Roosevelt said, "We are not prisoners of fate, but only prisoners of our mind." Public speaking success begins when we free our mind of negative thoughts and believe in possibilities.

Assert a Position
Anyone can be a public speaker and a decent one at that – if they learn and practice some key presentations skills and get out of their own way.

Think about your presentation, its objective and what you want the audience to remember and do when you are done speaking. Look at the detail you've organized into three key areas. Now think of an opening that would grab their attention.

Write your opening word-for-word:

_____

_____

_____

_____

_____

_____

Because many people are most nervous at the start of a presentation, and the start of the presentation sets the stage for audience attention, you want a smooth take-off.

Writing out your opening word for word and committing it to memory helps manage anxiety. This is the rare occasion where I sanction memorization. Repeating your memorized opening to yourself before you actually speak it aloud to a group, helps you get through the start-up jitters. Instead of focusing on thoughts of fear or discomfort, your attention is fully concentrated on the opening.

It's impossible to be thinking something fearful or negative at the same time you are saying your opening. So write out the first few sentences of your unique opening and commit it to memory or simply know and own how you will begin.

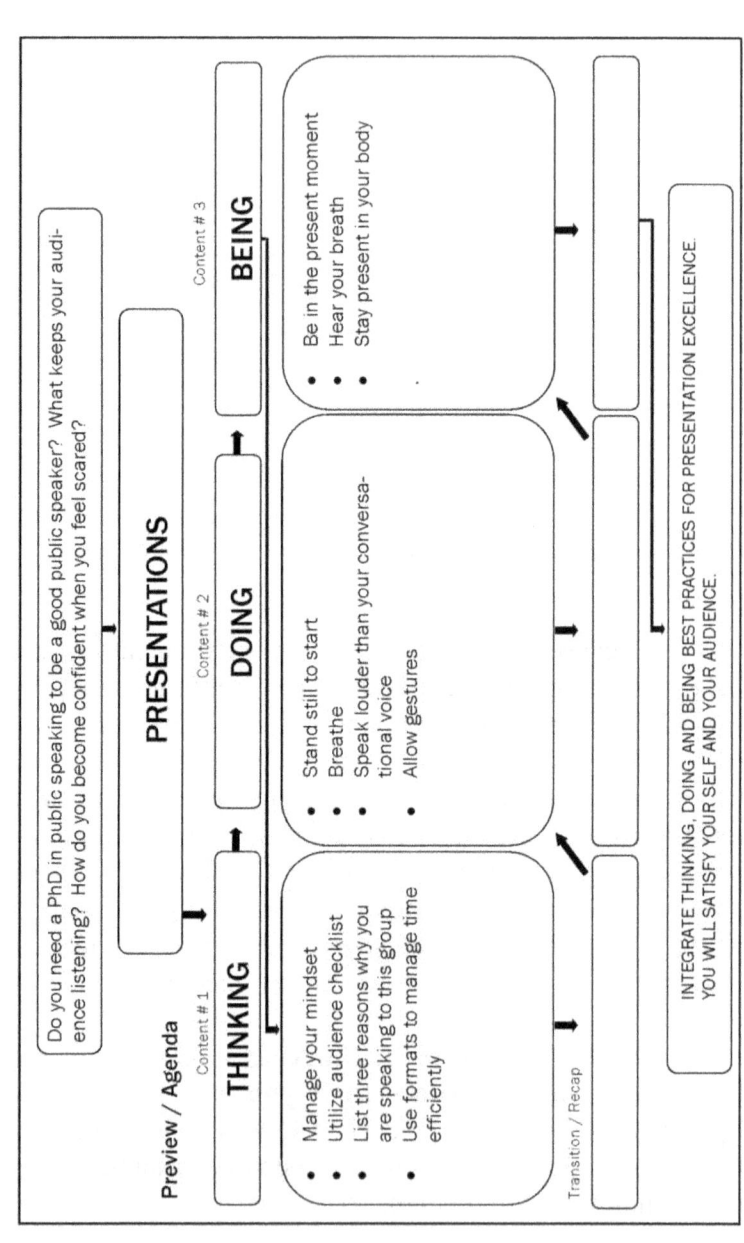

Figure 7.1 Format Worksheet

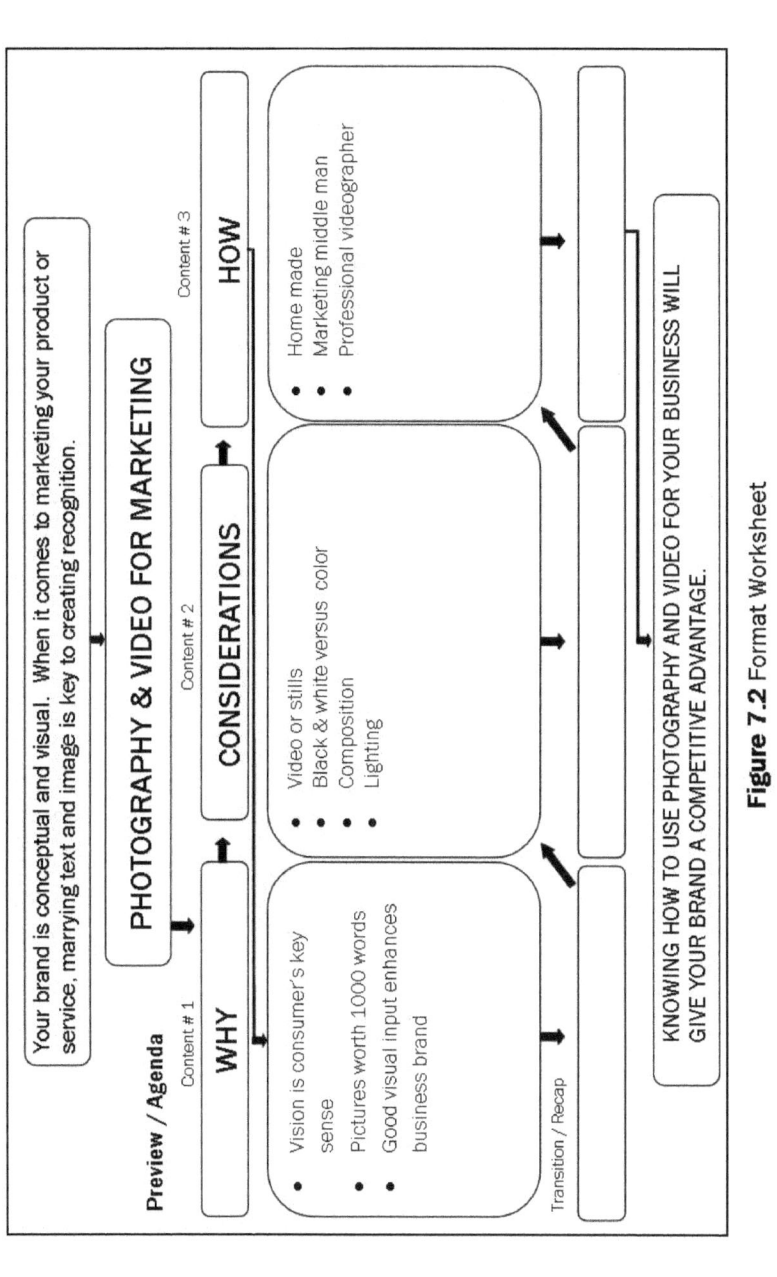

Figure 7.2 Format Worksheet

THINKING REVIEW

- ✓ Step 1: Manage Your Mindset
- ✓ Step 2: Answer Why YOU and Audience WHO
- ✓ Step 3: Turn Your Objective into a Conclusion
- ✓ Step 4: Brainstorm on Paper
- ✓ Step 5: Organize Content in 3's
- ✓ Step 6: Flesh Out and Fill In with Details
- ✓ Step 7: Create an Opening that Hooks

Chapter 8
Visual Aids: Stimulate or Complicate

Step 8: Reflect and Decide on Visual Aids

You don't have to use visual aids or PowerPoint slides to be a good presenter! Think about the great orators: Aristotle, Winston Churchill, Martin Luther King. Visual aids are a speaker's option, not a presentation prerequisite, and thus the last step of the Thinking phase.

Visual aids are meant to enhance your message, not *be* your message (nor obstruct or compete with your message!) Too many people rely on slides to tell their story. Click, talk, click, talk, click, talk. The audience becomes conditioned to look at the screen rather than engage with you when your visuals are out of balance with your verbal presentation.

While different types of presentations will use more or less slides, the case for using visual aids comes from these three facts:

- 70 percent of our information comes to us visually
- Images help people remember
- A presenter who uses visuals is perceived as more credible than one who does not use visuals

However beware: **Visual aids without a clear message can often create confusion for the audience.** They can negatively affect your credibility as well as distract your listeners from listening.

Think of your presentation as a story. You illustrate a story with pictures, but not every page has an illustration, and the book cannot be understood nor told by the images alone.

Think pictures, photos, graphs, charts, video, rather than words or text.

Most business presentations have slides with too much text. While some words can help to reinforce ideas and clarify details, sentences and paragraphs on slides is a formula for fatigue if not failure. After all, in speaking, your spoken words *are* your text.

So, once again, look at your format, your three areas of content and the detail you have chosen for those content areas. Reflect on **what content would be better remembered with an illustration, a picture or image. You can indicate that on your format by placing a square next to the information for which you will have an image.** See Figures 8.1 and 8.2 as examples.

CAUTION: Having a visual aid for every point you make can create a monotonous pattern! You can also create images using metaphors, stories and anecdotes.

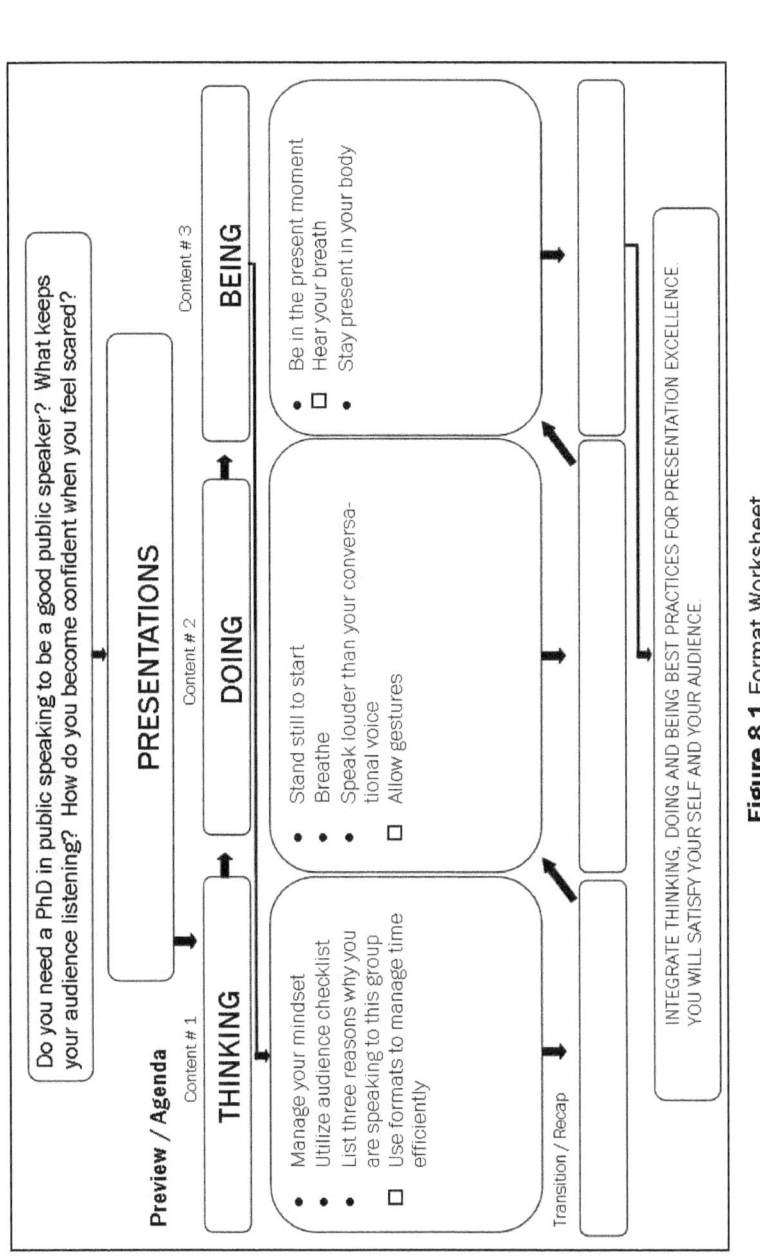

Figure 8.1 Format Worksheet

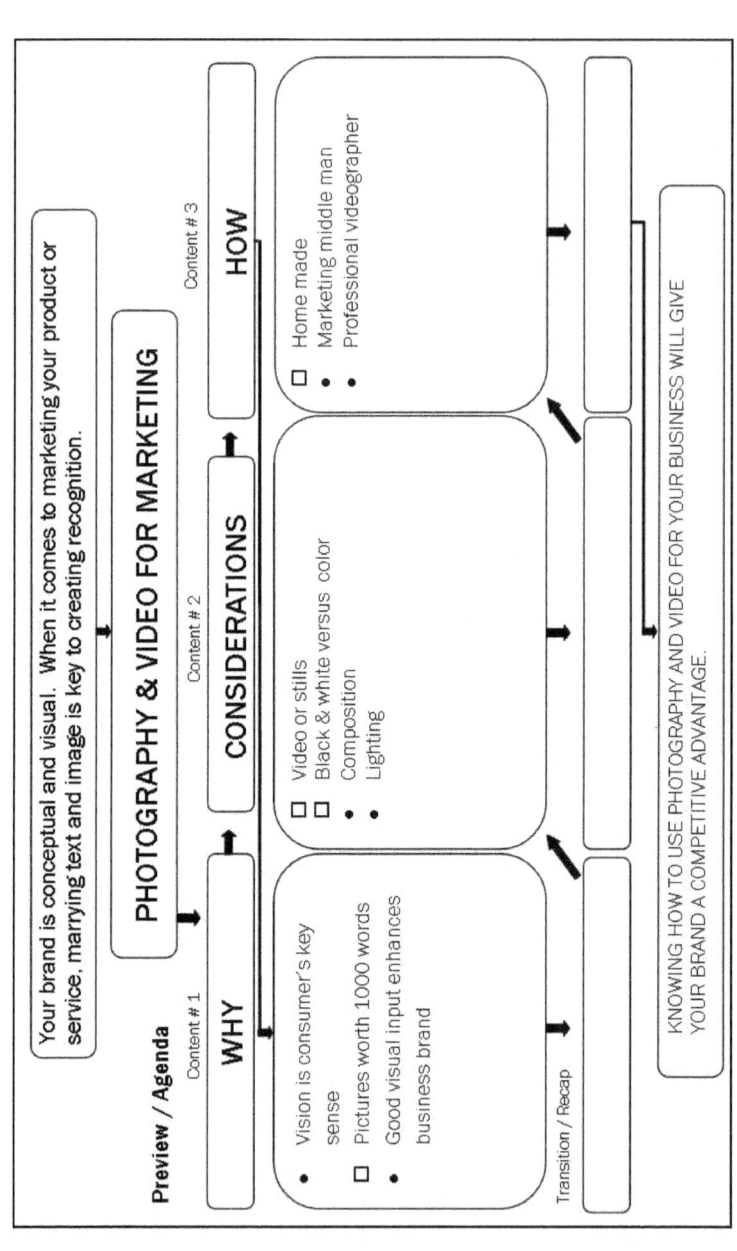

Figure 8.2 Format Worksheet

THINKING REVIEW

- ✓ Step 1: Manage Your Mindset
- ✓ Step 2: Answer Why YOU and Audience WHO
- ✓ Step 3: Turn your Objective into a Conclusion
- ✓ Step 4: Brainstorm on Paper
- ✓ Step 5: Organize your Content in 3's
- ✓ Step 6: Flesh Out and Fill In with Details
- ✓ Step 7: Create an Opening that Hooks
- ✓ Step 8: Reflect and Decide on Visuals

Chapter 9
Transitions: Content Linkage

Step 9: Construct Transitions

Now that you have determined your topic, conclusion, agenda, content landmarks, content detail, opening and visual support, you can add some linking language to smoothly transition from one content area to the next.

In my experience, when you rehearse your presentation for the first time aloud, you will either experience ease or awkwardness between your content areas. If after you present content one, you feel as though you hit a speed bump or dead end, you may want to write a sentence to effect a smooth transition between subtopics. If transitions come automatically as you rehearse your presentation aloud, you don't need to write anything more.

Here are some transition sentences to help with your content flow:

- So, now that you understand (Content 1), let's move on to (Content 2).
- To recap, (Content 1) is ... which leads me to my next point, (Content 2).
- (Content 1) is our critical first step. What do we need next? Let me tell you.

Look at figures 9.1 and 9.2 on the next two pages to understand how to format your transitions.

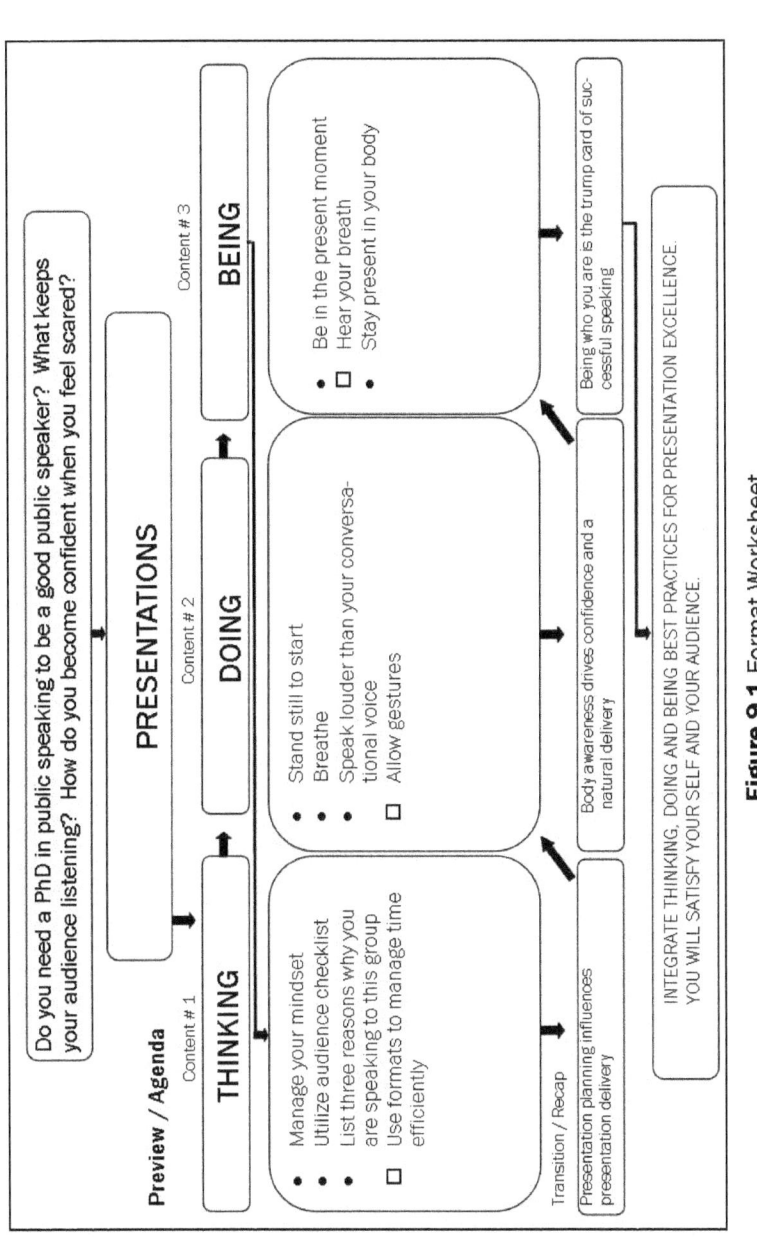

Figure 9.1 Format Worksheet

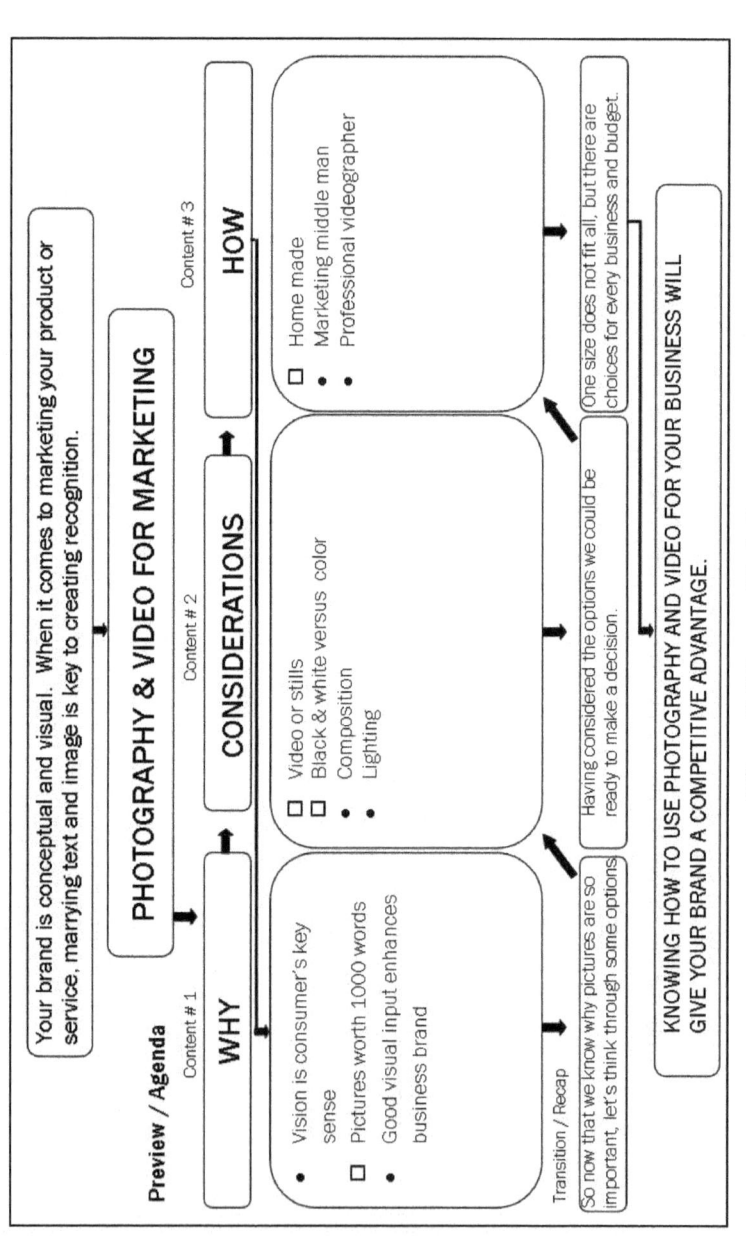

Figure 9.2 Format Worksheet

THINKING REVIEW

- ✓ Step 1: Manage Your Mindset
- ✓ Step 2: Answer Why YOU and Audience WHO
- ✓ Step 3: Turn your Objective into a Conclusion
- ✓ Step 4: Brainstorm on Paper
- ✓ Step 5: Organize your Content in 3's
- ✓ Step 6: Flesh Out and Fill In with Details
- ✓ Step 7: Create an Opening that Hooks
- ✓ Step 8: Reflect and Decide on Visuals
- ✓ Step 9: Construct Transitions

Chapter 10
Q&A: Anticipate and Abbreviate

Step 10: Reflect on and Answer Potential Questions

Sometimes presenters fall short of their presentation targets because they overlook planning for the Question and Answer period or Q&A. For some, there is a sigh of relief that they have gotten through their presentation alive! Others are simply satisfied they have delivered the message with clarity and confidence. In any case, though the formal and planned aspect of your presentation is finished (Presentation Part A), the full presentation is not complete until after you have asked your audience to participate. You do this by asking for questions. This is Part B of your presentation and an integral part of the entire presentation experience.

Reflecting on potential questions your audience might ask is a critical aspect of your presentation planning. What would *you* ask if you listened to your own presentation? What questions do you hope people will ask? What questions are you hoping *won't* be asked? Thinking about these questions and how you would respond to them **is** a way to prepare.

What are some questions that you think could be asked?

Question 1

___

___

___

Question 2

___

___

___

Question 3

___

___

___

Write your answers to these questions.

Answer to Question 1

___

___

___

Answer to Question 2

Answer to Question 3

THINKING REVIEW

- ✓ Step 1: Manage Your Mindset
- ✓ Step 2: Answer Why YOU and Audience WHO
- ✓ Step 3: Turn Your Objective into a Conclusion
- ✓ Step 4: Get Clear: Brainstorm on Paper
- ✓ Step 5: Organize Content in 3's
- ✓ Step 6: Flesh Out and Fill In with Details
- ✓ Step 7: Create an Opening that Hooks
- ✓ Step 8: Reflect and Decide on Visuals
- ✓ Step 9: Construct Transitions
- ✓ Step 10: Reflect on and Answer Potential Questions

Part II
THE DOING STAGE

*"I speak two languages,
body and English."*
Mae West

*"When you change your behavior, you change
your identity."*
Dan Millman

Chapter 11
Self Control and Other Control

It was in the beginning of my speaking career and I was on the agenda to speak to about a hundred soon-to-be entering college freshmen at Rutgers University. I was the last speaker of a three-day orientation process, it was 6:30PM on a hot August evening, and the air conditioning had died. Oh yes, the students were promised pizza at the end of my presentation.

I remembered my mentor's guidance about standing firm and speaking eye-to-eye. But what do you do when eyes are closed and heads are bowed in heat-exhaustion and end-of-event boredom? With a leap of faith, I placed my eyes on the bowed head of a student where the eyes might be if I drew a smiley face on his head. Then I talked to this place. Lo and behold! He raised his head. He felt my energy reaching out to him, personally. Now he was facing forward and I was no longer speaking to imaginary eyes atop his head but was directly engaged eye-to-eye. I saw another listless soul who was not facing forward. Again I talked to imaginary eyes and once again, I was immediately able to attract the listener's attention. Trust me. This practice works and it's amazingly fun to control a room by engaging with the audience deeply–one person at a time.

Become Conscious of Self; not Self-Conscious

While there is no one, "right" way to deliver a speech, there are techniques that support speaker confidence and audience attention. Just as with tennis or golf, there is a preferred way to place your body and hold your racket or club so you are more likely to play your best and to score. However, sometimes you can win even when your body weight and form are in less desirable positions. The same is true for presentations. Even when your body language is less than ideal, you can still satisfy your audience. Knowing which behaviors serve you and your audience and integrating them into your presentation repertoire over the long-term, will consistently help you manage performance anxiety, gain confidence, and influence audience buy-in.

People seem to be in constant motion even when they are presumably quiet and at rest. Without conscious awareness or intention, they are brushing aside a stray hair, readjusting a strap, craning their necks to stretch out a knot or shifting balance from one foot to the next. They are blinking, licking their lips, rubbing their eyes, steepling their fingers and jingling keys in their pockets. Listeners tend to either consciously or unconsciously overlook or react to these behaviors.

The movements we make are neither good nor bad. However, if you are the person at the front of the room and all eyes are on you, it's a good idea to know what you do that works and what you do that compromises your credibility and message. Humans are judgmental; they will naturally notice some mannerisms and judge yea or nay. You, the speaker can be forever fossilized as remote, haughty, nervous, stern, nerdy, or unprofessional because of one small, unconscious movement.

Remember, your audience is diverse. Some people will listen for ideas and substance, facts and figures, and proof and logic. Others will hope for enthusiasm, electricity, and excitement. In between will be listeners who are satisfied with plain and pleasant, while others will want eloquent and worldly. Despite this listening diversity, audiences as a rule, value a substantive message that is delivered with passion and confidence.

What do passion and confidence look like? From a behavioral perspective, what does this mean? What do you notice when you listen to a speaker? I value speakers who look natural and professional, self-aware but not self-conscious, who are attentive to their audience and who know how to actively engage them. Self-awareness of one's body helps the speaker manage extraneous nervous movement, which in turn supports listener attention.

Strong platform skills get audiences to focus on **what you say, rather than on how you look.** The goal is to neutralize distracting, unconscious mannerisms that can upstage your message and throw you off-balance.

Speaking of how you look, a friend said to me recently that there are three *You's*: the *You* reflected in the mirror, the *You* others see and the inner *You*. This underscores the importance of getting feedback about how you appear, especially when you are speaking before a group or the media. A disheveled hairdo, an askew tie, too much jewelry or make-up, a run in your stocking or wrinkled trousers can distract your audience from listening to your message. These minor things become magnified when an audience listens, but they are easily corrected. Ask someone you trust to look you over, making sure your teeth are spinach-free or there's no lipstick on your collar. You want your listeners focused on your message, and ensuring your image is poised and professional is the path to that destination.

Tweaking your body language, improving your image and slightly modifying your non-verbal behavior will serve you and your presentations going forward. You do not have to choreograph, act, or pretend. Instead, you become aware, adjust and adopt new behaviors that influence your physical presence.

In the next chapter, we'll take a look at specifics. There are five body elements to examine that are essential to improving your presentation performance. They are your feet, eyes, face, voice, and hands.

Chapter 12
Stand Still and Hold Your Ground

Body Language Best Practice 1:
Anchor your Feet

Your credibility as a speaker begins before you say a word. Audiences want visual satisfaction, even when they are not aware that they do. When 55 percent of your first impression results from your non-verbal behavior in the initial thirty to sixty seconds, why be a moving target, unbalanced sculpture, or antsy dancer?

Feet represent your stance, your ability to be solidly grounded, your posture, and your movement – walking, pacing, shifting, etc. Many speakers pay little if any attention to their feet. After all, the speaking focus is in the face, the mouth, the voice, and the words. But how many times have you been distracted by a speaker moving back and forth, side to side, cha-cha-cha? Maybe you have noticed the movement and ignored it, or maybe it became so distracting it compromised your ability to concentrate on the speaker's message. Audiences listen to presenters with their eyes as well as with their ears, so minimizing distracting movements is a key speaker responsibility.

To overcome the tendency for movement to lead you, start your presentation with conscious awareness of how you stand. Notice if you lean, fidget or pace. Do you rock on one heel and then the other? Do you sway side to side, pace the length of the stage or room, or sashay towards or away from your audience? It's best to know what you do so you realize what the audience sees. Then you can decide if this is behavior to change or ignore.

When it's time for the crowd to take you in, let them see you standing comfortably still. Do not misinterpret standing still as standing at attention. Comfortable standing control is the goal. But wait! You say, you're not comfortable standing still? You must move when you are nervous? You feel that movement lessens that anxious, uncomfortable feeling?

I hear you and I've heard this from many before. I've even said it myself. However, standing comfortably still is crucial and a skill easily learned. I would rather you have the choice of moving rather than defaulting to unconscious movement moving you! Are you afraid you can't learn to stand comfortably still for twenty seconds? Why not take the challenge?

Start your presentation grounded and still. In the first five, ten, fifteen, or twenty seconds of your speech, when your audience is most attentive and critical, be comfortably in control of your body stance and movement. You will look solid and professional, and this relaxed stillness will help you feel centered and calm and help your audience feel at ease as well. The audience will be looking at you and waiting for your words, just like an orchestra waits for the conductor's baton to signal the start of the music and the departure from silence.

The shorter your speech, the more important is the stillness. Making a toast that takes less than five minutes? Introducing a speaker at a networking function? Reading a passage from a prayer book at a religious ceremony? The human eye is drawn to movement. In a three-minute speech you want the audience to be "all ears." When your speech is brief, stay rooted.

Walk Without Talk Exercise

The following exercise will help you manage nervous and project strength.

Walk at a comfortable pace with a positive intention. Arrive at your destination and stop! Intentionally place your feet in a parallel position about shoulder width apart. This is a posture you may recognize from golf, tai chi, yoga, tennis, or skiing, to name a few. Feel your feet connect to the ground; feel both your heels and the balls of each foot contact the floor. This is more than just standing; it's conscious standing, with energy awareness in your feet. Make sure your knees are not locked; keep them relaxed and slightly bent, not stiff. Breathe consciously in this position, three or four full inhalations and exhalations. This is the posture that best supports the human structure and is your presentation starting point.

Override your tendency to move by energizing your feet and sensing your soles making contact with the floor. Continue breathing into this experience. When you are still, you have more inner control and the audience sees you looking calm. They cannot fault you for pacing, starting your talk as you're walking to your place in front of the group, or rocking on one heel. The audience takes in your personal stature and presence. They don't know what you're feeling or how hard you're working to become comfortably still. What they perceive is professional, neutral and acceptable. Managing your stance, anchoring your feet to support posture and presence, is one way to **gain control over what feels out of control.**

This practice takes practice. Minutes or hours over a week's time and you'll have this skill down pat. Standing still and anchoring your body is work, and an exercise that would be best learned before you get up to speak before a group. When you have integrated this behavior ahead of the time you need to use it, it becomes automatic. You walk in silence to your destination and position yourself to start.

Chapter 13
Eye Contact and Connection

Body Language Best Practice 2:
Connect with Your Audience One Person at a Time

With your feet comfortably planted, you manage nervous movement, project ease and confidence and establish your non-verbal credibility. Once you have settled into this quiet stance, it is time to actively engage your listeners. Just as credibility begins before you say a word, engaging your audience begins without sound.

Your eyes anchor you to your listener, just as your feet anchor your body to the ground. Eye contact is your most powerful non-verbal speaking tool. However, all eye contact is not the same, and becoming skilled at eye contact that makes connection is really the name of the game.

Some public speaking methods teach speakers to "eye-sweep" a room, like a surveillance camera. The eye-sweep method might work for formal audiences of hundreds or thousands, but it misses the mark for smaller audiences. Sweeping eye movement is impersonal and lacks connection. Additionally, it often causes the speaker to feel separate and disconnected.

Some speech coaches will ask you to focus your eyes on an individual's shoulder, eyeball a person's nose or look at the wall at the back of the room, the idea being that if you are too nervous to look at your audience, you can pretend you're looking at them. This is a silly suggestion if you ask me. Will looking at someone's shoulder or nose or at the wall behind them influence listening and attention? What can a shoulder, nose, or wall actually do? Will this satisfy your audience? Does looking outward in your audience's direction without actually engaging them personally give *you* any satisfaction?

Many people challenge the idea of speaking to individuals eye-to-eye. They have been taught "not to stare" and are uncomfortable looking directly into the eyes of people they don't know. They consider it rude and also argue that different cultures have different tolerances and rules for eye contact. I agree that staring is intrusive and I also know that eye contact has cultural nuances. However, eyes do more than stare. They smile, excite, wince, wink, squint, engage, and show compassion, interest, and aliveness. Engaging people eye-to-eye is non-negotiable. It is a must-do!

If looking at people makes you nervous, ask yourself why this is so. Do you want to feel this nervous feeling? Would you like to become naturally at ease connecting with an audience individual eye-to-eye? One-to-one eye contact for public speaking has extreme benefits for both listener and speaker.

What if you look at someone and she turns her gaze away? That certainly can happen and you should be prepared for that. Different people tolerate eye contact differently. That is their right and choice. You, as a speaker have the choice as well. You chose connection, and they chose not to connect. It's as though you are offering a gift and they are choosing not to receive it. Both are allowed. There are many people in the audience. All will not avert your gaze. Many of them will appreciate the individual attention. If you never risk deep eye-contact, you'll never know the gift that connection offers. **Err on the side of giving rather than avoiding when it comes to eye contact**.

However, to be effective and engaging, eye contact has to be comfortable. While people use eye contact regularly in their conversations or discussions, they are usually unconscious about how they use their eyes. They are mostly focused on what they are saying, not on how they are saying it. Most people learned eye contact covertly from parents or educators. A parent may have said, "Look at me when I talk to you" or a teacher or friend urged you to pay attention, meaning to listen and look simultaneously. Generally, eye contact has not been directly taught for any type of communication: conversation, discussion, or presentation.

Not until high school, college, or even employment do most people receive any formal public speaking eye contact training. To exacerbate the situation, training varies in quality and content. I can't count the number of times I've been asked at a presentation seminar whether a speaker should imagine his audience naked or sitting on the toilet. Would that make you comfortable? Why would you want to see naked bodies of all sorts and sizes, genitals, breasts, buttocks, bellies during your presentation? Hey, if it works for you, by all means, do what works. But in my opinion this is counterintuitive and would be a huge distraction for most!

One-on-one eye contact is best for talking to groups. It's not just looking at a pair of eyes, like looking at a picture on the wall, however. It is eye connection, using your eyes to engage the other energetically, emotionally and cognitively.

Consider your eyes like the prongs of a plug and an audience participant's eyes as a socket. Plug in and connect before you speak your words. If you have really plugged in and made a connection, you can feel that energy of connection. However, if you're stingy with your eyes and only cursorily skim those of your listeners, you will not feel much of anything. Have you ever plugged in your radio, hairdryer, or electric shaver only to realize the prongs were not solidly making a connection? The appliance did not work, did it? Without the full connection, there was no current, no energy flow.

Fully connect with your eyes before you say a word. This is powerful human technology and I've seen this in action. I've practiced it, fumbled it a bit in my first few speeches, and honed this skill so it is what I now do naturally all the time. By connecting non-verbally eye-to-eye, you influence audience attention. Your energy magnetizes the listeners' energy. It's so easy and unbelievably powerful!

The goal is to engage as many individuals as you can. That is your intention. Each person whose eyes connect with you is more likely to listen to your message, even if it's not their point of view. When you have the intention to communicate to individuals rather than to a "group" your eye contact is more personal and intimate. Individuals in the audience feel this intimacy and, being human, respond favorably. If you treat a group generically, you put your influence at risk. **Bottom line: treat the group as individual listeners and your influence increases**.

And, yes, there will be times when speaking one-to-one to every person in the room might be impossible. Consider a stage environment where there are thousands in your audience. It is very unlikely that you will eye-connect to each and every one of your listeners. However, you can stretch your gaze to different areas of the audience with the intent to connect with those people in a particular segment of the room.

In large groups such as this, I mentally divide the room into **a tic-tac-toe board so there are nine distinct areas**. I target left rear, front center, mid-right, front-left, mid-rear. Get the picture? So will the audience. They may not be conscious of your eye-connecting intention, but they probably will appreciate it. People like the feeling of connection; it's built into being human.

Here's one more thought about eye contact that relates to the physiology and function of the human eye.

We tend to take "looking" for granted. But looking at an inanimate object is different than looking at a videotape, a quarterback running down the football field, a couple dancing or an audience.

Eye physicians and visual specialists know what I am talking about I'm sure. But most of us rarely give looking a second thought, or consider the different muscle adjustments that affect our visual process as we gaze, see, focus, or perceive.

Eye Exercises for Engagement Excellence
1. Exercise for targeting and shifting direction

Go into a room, perhaps your living room or den. Intentionally look at a chair for three seconds. Keeping your body stationary, look at a picture on the wall. Hold that gaze for three seconds. Now find a lamp and focus your eyes on it for three seconds. Be sure you are standing still. **You can move your eyes without moving your lower body.**

2. Exercise for voice and eyes

Use the same objects in the room and count aloud to five as you look at each one. Target the chair, breathe and count to five. Shift your gaze in silence and count from five to ten as you look at a picture, and eleven to fifteen when you look at the lamp. **Do not count when you shift your gaze. You must land your eyes on the object before you begin counting.**

3. Exercise for connection with a pretend audience

Arrange chairs as in an audience. Place dolls, stuffed animals, or attach images of people. Sub-vocally, speak the name of the object or picture in the chair, and speak a sentence to the pretend listener. For example, *Bear, how are you? Doll, did you know I..., Mr. President, the motivation for this research...etc.*

As an adaptation of the above, eliminate the name of the object, and engage the "chair," which represents a listener, with a part of a nursery rhyme, poem, or the words to a song. Then shift your gaze in silence to another chair, lock in with the object and add another stanza of the rhyme, poem, or song. Continue to engage the objects one at a time. Once you feel the timing of these practice exercises, you can substitute impromptu speaking, your speech outline, or the full speech itself. These exercises train your eyes to focus before speaking and reinforce the intimacy of one-to-one eye contact.

If you commit to connecting to people, not noses or walls, and take the three to six seconds of time it takes to really connect, you will realize that speaking to individuals is the only way to speak. Practice these eye skills and presentation comfort will soon be yours.

Chapter 14
Smile: A Non-Verbal Social Lubricant

Body Language Best Practice 3:
Energize Your Face and Mouth

We know that your demeanor, before you speak, speaks volumes. Your size, shape, race, gender, clothes, posture, stance, facial features, and expression are non-verbal elements that audiences observe and possibly judge – good, bad, or indifferent.

Let's say you are out at a pub or cafe. How do you initially meet someone? What happens first? Initially, you see a person or look in their direction, right? What happens next? Possibly, you smile. You might be smiling with your eyes at first, and then you may feel a bit more comfortable and decide to be more open. The muscles at the corners of your mouth begin to energize and lift, creating a smile. A smile is a great nonverbal tool for making a friend, meeting a new dating prospect, and engaging an audience. It communicates friendliness and most human beings appreciate this overture.

Before you speak, as you stand comfortably still, looking, engaging eye-to-eye with an individual - smile! It's an ice-breaker for both you and your audience!

Chapter 15
Voice: Lullaby, Dirge, or Infomercial?

Body Language Best Practice 4:
Project and Animate Your Voice

Your voice is the carrier of your words. Without voice you might have speech, but no sound. Without voice, your words will not be heard, your message will not be processed and you will obviously lack influence.

On numerous occasions, people have complained to me about their voices. Many are self-critical: *I don't like my voice. It sounds too young. It quivers too much. It sounds whiney, raspy, tense, like my mother's, or father's, or brother's, etc.* It's important to hear a client's concern about his voice and to provide training and support if needed. It's just as important to discriminate between vocal dislike, vocal dysfunction, and vocal health.

Disliking one's voice often relates more to psychological issues than to physiological ones. Emotional aspects of voice need to be addressed for the person's overall personal growth and well-being. If disliking your healthy and normal voice causes you unhappiness or interferes with your ability to feel comfortable speaking to groups, then consider the professional services of a voice coach, speech therapist, or counselor.

However, for presenters with normal vocal structure and function, there are three key vocal practices to embrace. Presenters will need to project to be heard, speak with articulation that's easy to understand, and speak at a speed that promotes audience comprehension.

If you are going to speak, speak so people can hear you. Do not muffle, whisper, or hide behind your hands. Projecting your voice is important and a courtesy to your listeners; they should not have to strain to hear you.

You cannot rely upon a conversational voice when speaking to a group greater than twenty-five to thirty. How much volume will depend on the room size, its acoustics, the furnishings, and the number of people in it. For a room of thirty to fifty people for example, speak about six times the volume of your normal, conversational voice. For most speakers, this adjustment happens quite naturally.

For example, when your five-year-old runs after a ball that's gone into the street, you use your voice to yell and warn him to be careful. When your team scores a goal or run, you may cheer with increased enthusiasm and volume. When talking in a noisy environment, you intensify your voice automatically. Most people don't know what they do on a physiological level to increase their volume, but they do know how to raise their voices.

Speak up to be heard and you will support your audience's ability to concentrate on your message. You will also energize yourself and minimize the tendency to get too relaxed, which can result in a trailing voice that becomes less audible over time. How do you learn voice projection?

Learn about breathing! Where there is voice, there is breath. The two are intrinsically linked. Hold your breath. Now try to speak. Impossible, right?

We rarely have to focus on our breath, though we may in fact breathe shallowly or not fully. Intentionally take a deep breath while focusing your eyes at the far end of the room, preferably connecting to a person. Hold the breath for one second before speaking. Your voice will be louder when you speak. This is a simple exercise for voice projection awareness. However, you will need to repeat and practice this exercise to sustain projection. I highly recommend working with a speech or voice coach or speech therapist with a specialization in voice, if you need to improve voice projection.

There are many books on voice with voice exercises, and they all begin with understanding breath and your breathing physiology: lungs, vocal cords, and the areas of the body that resonate sound. Some very simple and fundamental exercises to begin the practice of breath awareness follow.

Breath Exercise 1 – Follow Your Breath

Sit comfortably in a chair with legs uncrossed. Put all your attention on your inhalation. Follow it until it naturally becomes an exhalation. Refrain from thinking. Turn off the mental chatter and simply follow your breath. Set a timer for two minutes and when your concentration shifts from breath to mind, stop and start the timer over. Note how you feel about becoming breath-conscious. Do you feel any resistance to sitting quietly and just listening to the sound of your breath? Can you lessen this resistance?

Breath Exercise 2: Manage your Breath – Seated

Again, sit comfortably in a chair or in a cross-legged position on the floor. Inhale consciously for six counts and then hold your breath before exhaling to six counts as well. Do this ten times.

Now intentionally inhale to four counts, hold your breath for four counts, and lengthen your exhale to eight counts. Do this several times. Can you stay focused on your breathing without thinking about things to do? Are you able to extend the exhalation?

Breath Exercise 3: Manage your Breath – Standing

Stand with feet parallel, knees slightly bent. Breathe naturally for several breaths. Now put your inner focus on following your breath as in the first exercise. Then switch to the second exercise, first managing the inhalation and exhalation equally, and then lengthening the exhalation following the holding or stopping of your breath.

Now do the above three exercises again, this time, focusing your eyes outward on an object or person, while your inner focus follows the course of your inhalation and exhalation.

Monotone and Inflection

Besides vocal projection, there are other vocal challenges that either empower or detract from your speaking. Limited vocal variety or intonation is one of them. Reduced intonation is commonly referred to as a monotone. Speakers from different language and cultural backgrounds may speak English with different intonation patterns. However, a monotonous voice can also be attributed to personality types and emotional issues. While everyone's tolerance for vocal variety differs, it's generally an audience preference to listen to a speaker who demonstrates some vocal variety.

Intonation Exercise 1

Practice the sentences below aloud, first speaking them robotically and monotonously. This is called negative practice. The premise behind this exercise is that if you can intentionally do something considered wrong, you have more control to create a contrast and shape a new behavior. After you read in a monotone, read the sentences again in a silly sing-song or up and down manner. The goal here is variability within your control, so don't judge, just play.

- What do you want?
- Please pass the potatoes.
- When are Uncle Sam and Aunt Betty visiting?
- I passed my examination in psychology but I received a low grade in math.

Intonation Exercise 2

Emphasizing different words in sentences is another exercise that influences intonation. Read the following and emphasize the underscored word. Listen for the differences in tone and emphasis.

- I <u>must</u> go home for lunch.
- I must go <u>home</u> for lunch.
- I must go home for <u>lunch</u>.
- The gray <u>cat</u> tried to scratch me.
- The <u>gray</u> cat tried to scratch me.
- The gray cat tried to scratch <u>me</u>.
- My <u>best</u> friend hates to wear stockings.
- <u>My</u> best friend hates to wear stockings.
- My best friend <u>hates</u> to wear stockings.

Intonation Exercise 3

Say the word "OH" in different ways to suggest the following meanings:

- Joy
- Fear
- Sympathy
- Amazement
- Doubt
- Curiosity
- Anger
- Disgust

Intonation Exercise 4

Read the words on the following page aloud, using appropriate inflection. The sentences in parentheses will help you determine a specific meaning for each word.

- So (We've caught you at last, you crook!)
- So (What's it to you?)
- Beth (Is that you?)
- Beth (What do you mean by sneaking in?)
- Stop here (Are you sure?)
- Stop here (At once!)
- Gary (Who?)
- Gary (That's who)
- Help! (I'm sinking)
- Help? (Why should I?)

Speaking too Fast

Another vocal pitfall that can cause an audience to stop listening is speaking too fast. Speak too quickly and you can compromise the clarity of your words and sound slurred or mumbled. After all the hard work of packaging your message, you don't want to fall prey to sloppy speech.

The best speech rate exercise I know has more to do with your eyes than with either your mouth or mind. Become an expert at one-to-one eye contact, always connecting non-verbally before engaging your mouth to speak, and you will automatically improve your public speaking rate. Inserting pauses is a best practice to modify speech rate without distorting the fluidity of your words and sentences.

Another exercise for managing speech rate involves listening. Most speakers are so focused on their words, that they barely hear what they say. Their thoughts flow from mind to mouth and out to the audience's ears. Become your own listener. Let your thoughts flow to your mouth, but hear them as you speak. This monitoring skill will impact your speaking in a positive way and also slow down your too rapid rate.

Articulation

If you lack speech clarity or your speaking muscles tire easily and compromise your message, you can try the following exercises. Tongue twisters are phrases and sentences that challenge the precision and coordination of the speech muscles.

Exercise 1: Tongue Twisters

Practice these sentences slowly at first and then increase your speed, always preserving accuracy over rate.

- Red rubber baby buggy bumpers
- Toy boat
- What noise annoys an oyster? A noisy noise annoys an oyster.
- I saw the six thick thumbs.
- Guy Gargoyle, Girl Gargoyle
- Abominable abdominal
- Sixteen stainless steel twin-screw cruisers
- The seething sea ceaseth – it sufficeth sufficiently that the seething sea ceaseth.

Articulation Exercise 2: Over-articulation

Take a paragraph from a book or newspaper and over-articulate or exaggerate each word as you read the paragraph aloud. This will sound stilted and unnatural. The exaggerated movements help strengthen and coordinate the muscles involved in speaking: particularly the lips, jaw, and tongue.

Remember: speech is a muscular activity, as is tennis, dancing, or yoga. If you exercise your speech muscles, you can improve speech function and clarity.

Hesitations, Um's and Uh's

Many speakers criticize their speaking because it is peppered with filler vocalizations, such as uh's and um's. While I value smooth and articulate speech, focusing on these *pausal markers* can be counterproductive. Unless a speaker routinely voices these sounds in some patterned way, for example, at the beginning of every third sentence, or at the start of every slide, the audience usually ignores them. A good speaker may have some hesitations in his speaking. If the overall speech is strong and the presenter is dynamic and connected with his audience, these little imperfections go unnoticed.

Rather than focus on these vocal placeholders, focus on delivering your speech as best you can. Get good at your talk, and then as a final finishing touch, you can address these little sounds.

I strongly recommend avoiding counting uh's and um's for a beginning speaker, perfectionist or a speaker of English as a Second Language. Too much attention on these small sounds can exacerbate speech anxiety, increase the number of hesitations going forward, and even have a long-lasting traumatic impact on a speaker's self-esteem and self-expression.

A professional speech coach employs strategies to strengthen and enhance fluency with an unwavering focus on building each individual's presentation confidence. Eliminating empty vocalizations is important and necessary for media presentations and for professional speakers, but I suggest putting your attention there only after you have developed a certain level of public speaking comfort and confidence, not at the beginning of your public speaking training.

Chapter 16
Absolutely Say Yes to Gestures

Body Language Best Practice 5:
Befriend Your Hands; Allow Natural Gestures

What do I do with my hands? is probably the question I'm asked most in presentation training courses. Many people try to control their hands and arms from moving. On more than a few occasions I have had to beg clients to embrace (no pun here) their gestures. *I'm Italian, so I speak with my hands. I hear that's bad. I try to keep them still, but I can't. I'm Jewish, I speak with my hands, I'm too expressive, etc.*

Well here's the deal. You have hands and they gesture in a way that's natural for *you*. Controlling your hands is not recommended! Allowing your gestures to be, is. There is a great degree of variety in gestures because they are related to gender, age, family, ethnicity, and personality. What's important is to be comfortable in your own skin and to allow your unique expression and animation to emerge.

By the way, your gestures and voice are physically linked. The more you project and feel passionate about your subject, the more likely you will gesture – and gesture naturally! Less vocal energy generally means less animation. Your goal is to allow what is true to your nature, no matter what your nationality or ethnicity.

Gestures will be appreciated differently by different people. People with low gesturing backgrounds may appreciate less gesture, or, wanting to be more expressive themselves, may prefer more expressiveness. You won't know what everyone thinks and it is definitely not your job to micro-manage or choreograph your hands.

Your goal is to feel comfortable with who you are and let your voice lead your hands naturally.

Here are a few tips on gestures:

Gesture Tip 1:

Your hands, like your feet, start in stillness. Before you speak, allow your hands to rest naturally at your sides. Inhibit the inclination to place your hands in your pockets, cross them over your chest or behind your back, or clasp them folded at your crotch. When hands are touching your body they draw attention away from your face, where eye engagement, speech, voice, and your message originate. If you don't want people looking at your chest, pelvis, or hips please let your arms and hands rest quietly at your sides. This starting position for your hands is *neutral*. It does not trigger judgments as do other gestural postures.

I can hear the pushback from some readers already. *That's weird. That's not natural. I'll look stiff ... etc.* Trust that your excitement will flow to your voice and energize your hands naturally and authentically.

Actually it takes more energy to unlock clasped hands or to uncross arms than to just allow gestures to happen. The last thing you want is for your gestures to get stuck in one place. You will feel awkward and not yourself without your gestures working in their own unique way.

Gesture Tip 2:

Gesture with your arms not your fingers! Have you ever seen someone with their arms at their sides, soldier-at-attention style, fingers wiggling around? This movement drew your attention and perhaps compromised listening fully to the speaker's words.

Make a commitment to learn how to stand with feet planted and arms comfortably at your sides – in neutral.

Breathe through the awkward feeling. Hold this position and concentrate on the inhalation and exhalation cycle of three full breaths. Do this daily and by the end of the week this new posture will no longer feel awkward. Challenge yourself to integrate this body language best practice into your non-verbal repertoire. The audience will view you positively and your confidence will grow!

What about media presentations, such as webinars and video-teleconferencing? When you are on television or a video-teleconference, you are generally seen from the waist up. The view is short and close as compared to a live standing presentation. Consequently, gestures will appear more defined. Absolutely allow for gestures and realize that standing space differs from seated space and will create a different view of your gestural communication. Just be careful that your gestures do not obscure your face.

Capitalize on these body language guidelines to manage nervousness and control non-verbal behavior that distracts your audience from listening to what you have to say. You are the medium for your message; the package of your point of view. Make it a strong and attractive one.

Body Language Best Practice Review

1. **Anchor your feet and stand still to start.** Let your audience take you in. Control of your stance prevents energy from leaking into nervous movement. It enhances your being grounded, so energy flows where it needs to go: to your voice, to your message to your audience.
2. **Engage and make eye contact, one person at a time.** Receive (not stare down) the person in silence. Then serve them your message, focusing on their taking it in. Really *see* them. A quick glance is not the same as a real connection. Err on the side of depth.
3. **Befriend with your face** – smile! A smile energizes your face and engages the audience. Create a connection and put your audience at ease by being proactively personal.
4. **Breathe and project so your voice can be heard.** The bigger the room, the bigger the breath. Practice your presentation opening in a volume that is comfortably loud for the size of the room.
5. **Gesture without judgment, naturally, and organically**. Your hands will move if you keep them unlocked and available and if you project your voice fully. Aside from starting in neutral, do not control your gestures, let them do their thing. They are an integral part of the human system and they will serve you if you allow them to just be.

Chapter 17
The Q&A: When Monologue Becomes Dialogue

There are a few body language considerations for managing an effective Question and Answer period. Let's consider the following.

You finish your last slide, summarize, and breathe a sigh of relief that the presentation is over. Since asking for questions is often expected, you routinely and hurriedly ask, "Are there any questions?" Seeing no hands, you thank your audience and leave the spotlight. This is typical behavior for many presenters. And it represents a missed opportunity.

The Question and Answer period is the Part B of your presentation. Until the Q&A, you have one hundred percent of the speaking responsibility and your audience has the full responsibility of listening. If you have crafted your message with your audience in mind, organized your presentation to have the right amount of detail, and executed the delivery with minimal distractions and just enough visual support, you will have engaged your audience's attention and influenced their listening.

The Q&A is when you shift from monologue to dialogue. Now is the time to engage your audience verbally. You want their questions. Questions move your message forward because listeners have now taken your message literally into their mouths. The audience talking about your message stimulates their ownership of it, and ownership moves your ideas towards action.

Some audience participants will want clarification of ideas you mentioned. Others will want validation that they understood your message correctly. And some, tired of listening, may be itching to be heard so badly that their style may teeter on a takeover.

Q& A Tip 1: How should I ask for questions?

It's quite natural and common to ask, "Do you have any questions?" However this type of question implies a yes or no response. A better way to frame a question is to ask the following:

What questions do you have about_____? Or, what questions can I answer or clarify for you? You can also ask a question that leads the crowd to a specific or additional point you want to emphasize by asking, *"What additional questions do you have about_____? (phase two, the leadership, project deadline, costs, etc.)*

Q&A Tip 2: What do I do if there are no questions?

If you ask for questions and no one offers one, it does not necessarily mean the audience has none. Sometimes, participants don't want to be the first to raise their hand or voice their concern. They may feel shy or fear that their questions aren't smart enough. Or, a participant might have a question, but concerned that the information might have already been covered, prefer to remain silent and avoid potential embarrassment. Basically, people do not want to feel foolish, so they refrain from asking questions.

If you do not receive a response to your first request for questions, ask and answer a question yourself. For example, you might say something like: *Some people may want to know why... Or, sometimes people have questions about how much time this process takes.* Ask the question and then answer it. Then follow with: *What other questions can I answer?*

Q&A Tip 3: How do I engage the whole audience?

Many of us have been taught that it is polite to look at the person who is talking to you. Most of us do that quite naturally in conversations. However, when responding to a questioner in groups, both formal and informal, there are some preferred techniques. Always listen to the question fully and give soft eye contact to the questioner. Refrain from any facial reactions that might indicate you are straining to understand or disagree with the questioner. Pause before you start your answer or if necessary, paraphrase the question to ensure that others in the room have heard the question too.

Begin answering the question to the questioner, giving the questioner full eye contact. Engage and connect with this person for a few sentences, and then **share the rest of your response with others in the audience,** one person at a time, similar to how you presented your prepared presentation. It is important to share your eye contact to more than the questioner for several reasons:

- You want to continue to engage the full audience and manage the energy in the room
- You want to avoid sidebars that cause the rest of the audience to lose interest
- You want to assume this question is one that others will want to hear

Q&A Tip 4: How do I handle difficult questioners?

Sometimes you will have a difficult person in the audience who may be adversarial or want attention and attempts to hog the question-asking floor. Unless you are aware, you may contribute to this dynamic. To avoid getting into a one-on-one sidebar with a questioner, especially if there is an edge or negative attitude, intentionally do not give the questioner eye contact. It is difficult to ask a question when the speaker has stopped looking at you. This skill does take practice, but it's a skill well worth learning. Recently, a seminar participant said that he once had a person in his audience talk right over him, despite his not giving the listener any eye contact. In this case, you might use a non-verbal technique such as a gesture that says "hold that thought" or move uncomfortably close to that person. You then can say something like: *I see you have a lot of questions on this matter. We have time restraints here, but let's meet afterwards so I can make sure your questions are answered.*

Q&A Tip 5: How do I answer difficult questions?

At least one in ten presenters ask: *What do I do if I don't know the answer to a question?* It is obvious and quite simple. Be honest, admit you don't have the answer and offer to find the information and communicate it to the questioner at a future date. If you promise to give someone additional information, do so promptly. Follow up with the information within forty-eight to seventy-two hours. **It is professional to say** *I don't know and I'll find out.* **It's unprofessional to pretend to know and fudge your response.**

Q&A Tip 6: How do I end the Q & A?

My favorite Q & A practice is to restate your conclusion when there are no more questions from the audience. Instead of saying thank you for your questions and leaving the presentation spotlight, end your presentation by reiterating your conclusion. This is the message you want to leave the audience with, not the answer to the last question.

The bottom line is: repeat your conclusion after all questions are answered and have the final word!

Chapter 18
Coordinating Visual Aids with Speaking

Once upon a time there were presentations without visual aids. Life was simple. Images were not projected upon a screen nor messages previewed in written form as handouts. Speakers spoke and audiences listened. That experience is now rare. Business presentations have become a speech type in a category all its own.

Since the 1980s a speech assisted by electronic, computerized visual aids has become the standard. In fact, event planners seem to assume that text and image are part and parcel of addressing a group. Keynote speakers and conference speakers are asked to forward their PowerPoint slides more than a month in advance of the actual speaking event! Conference attendees receive a three-inch thick binder of slide reprints before the speaker even says his first word. The audience looks at the notes as the speaker speaks or reads. Only the rare keynote, inspirational leader, or comic is given any visual aid slack. In almost all other situations, there is the expectation that to be fully understood, speakers must include visual aids in their presentation.

You may be thinking that I'm the visual aid vigilante, but that's not the case at all. I am simply against the notion that having them is imperative, as if speaking without pictures is second-class or wrong. I'm all in favor of visual aids if they are indeed visual and if they assist the audience in better understanding the speaker's message. Visual aids when thoughtful and thought-out are great for both speaker and audience.

Benefits of Visual Aids

The key reason for using visual aids is to influence understanding and support message retention. Since 75 percent of what we know comes to us through visual channels, it follows that visual representation of a speaker's words can support audience understanding.

Other benefits to incorporating visual aids into your presentations are:

- Support visual learners
- Stimulate interest in a subject
- Reinforce what has been said.
- Reduce the time required to present a concept
- Enhance the audience's perception of the speaker

Unfortunately, most presentations have visual aids that are cluttered, distracting, and confusing. Instead of the speaker's message becoming clearer, the "aids" muddy the waters. Slides are crammed with sentences that are the textual equivalent of the speakers' words. Too many times the speaker reads these words, so there is more reading than speaking. The visual aids no longer reinforce the message; they become the message.

Visual Aids that Work

Effective visual aids utilize image and color to illustrate the speaker's concepts. As with storybooks, cookbooks, and biographies, where not all pages have illustrations, presentations do not require images for everything spoken. Like spices, visual aids should be used sparingly, lest they become overbearing. You want the seasoning to enhance the main course, not *be* the main course (how satisfied would you be eating cumin, curry, or tarragon straight from the spice jar)?

To enhance an audience's attention and support presentation processing, visual aids need to be **simple, colorful, and pictorial**. Rather than words or text, consider incorporating the following:

- Clip art
- Photographs
- Video segments
- Graphs
- Charts
- Symbols ($, %)

You certainly can use text, but the balance of text and image must favor the latter. A suggested guideline is the 6x6 rule. This means that on any slide, there are only six lines of text with no more than six words per line.

When a presenter uses visual aids sparingly and effectively, the audience is more likely to leave the presentation room remembering the speaker's message.

Managing Visual Aids

The twin to effective visual aid design is effective visual aid management. Strong visuals with poor execution will weaken the visual's impact and possibly ruin the speaker's presentation. An audience is more likely to remember the delay caused by a computer glitch, the speaker's frustration, or fumbled visual aid mechanics, than the presentation content.

I remember my first presentation using visual aids. In the 1980's, I was nervous. I didn't feel confident doing two things at once, speaking and changing slides. Actually these were overhead transparencies. I knew the material, but felt clumsy at coordinating the visuals with my speaking. I can't stress enough how important it is to practice this multi-tasking before your actual presentation event.

There are many intelligent professionals who present well but whose credibility is tainted by their under-practiced execution of visual aid mechanics. The following are some common visual aid pitfalls:

- Reading the slides word for word
- Looking at the slides instead of the audience
- Standing in the light of the projector
- Pointing to the slide
- Tracking or tracing an image (graph line) on a slide
- Advancing a slide too soon
- Not advancing a slide soon enough
- Talking too much while the audience processes the slide
- Letting the slide lead the presentation story

You can see from this list that these problems fall into three main categories:

1. Reading vs. speaking
2. Managing space
3. Managing time

Reading Slides

Eliminating slide reading is a frequent coaching request. Corporations want confident leaders who project executive presence. **Reading dilutes speaker presence**. This is because the speaker is engaged with his text rather than individuals in the audience. You cannot be connecting eye-to-eye if you're using your eyes to read. Some speakers report feeling left out of their own presentations and as a result of reading, disconnected from their audience.

When you are speaking and your audience is reading, your presentation timing is out of sync with the audience, and you put your connection and credibility at risk. This is easily rectified, however, by balancing your speaking with your watching, reading, and processing.

Wouldn't it be better to proactively stop talking, show a slide, watch the audience as they process it, and see them get it? Don't we pause to look at the pictures in a storybook?

The best practice to overcome slide reading is to say what you want to say, pause while noticing the audience read and process the information on the screen, and then, seeing that they have done so, continue with your story. This process eliminates the all-too-familiar situation of speaking to an audience who is reading your slide.

Unique Situations for Reading your Slides

Reading slides is often good if you are quoting someone and want to emphasize *their* words. For international audiences, you may expand this practice, since reading is often a more developed second language skill than listening. However, I prefer that speakers read less and pause more, giving space for the audience to read. Many people are insulted when you read what they can read themselves!

Looking at Slides vs. Looking at Your Audience

A close cousin to reading your slides is looking at your slides. Humans are physiologically drawn to image and light, so no matter how charismatic you are, your projected visuals, both good and bad, will draw your audience away from you. When you are talking and your own eyes are oriented to your slides, you, like your audience, have been trapped by the power of illumination, color, and shape. Although you are not reading what is projected, you are unconsciously magnetized and often anchored to the screen. Instead of engaging and connecting with your audience holistically – using your eye contact, posture, voice, gestures and message in an integrated way – you have been pulled into and become at the effect of your support materials.

To overcome the tendency to speak to your slides, speak only when you have engaged a listener eye-to-eye. If you follow this practice, your ability to sustain an audience's attention will skyrocket.

Unique Situations for Looking at your Slides

You might *plan* to look at your slides in some specific cases. For example, if you have projected a complicated chart or graph, you may choose to minimize your presence by withdrawing eye contact from the audience. Instead, you **intentionally** look at the slide which focuses the audience's attention to where you are looking. This is similar to what weather reporters on television do.

The departure from being fully focused on your audience signals the audience that something very important needs to be looked at–literally! However, you do not stay glued to your visuals. To be effective, this shift from connecting to the audience to looking at a slide needs to be brief. Moreover, since you have planned this shift, you are in control of this plan. You are not at the effect of the illuminated screen. Done well and not too often, this is a very effective technique.

Managing Visual Aids and Space – Standing in the Light of the Projector

If you want to instantly lose credibility, stand in the light of the projector. Your human shadow on the screen will obscure the data and images that were designed to support your talk. You can get away with this once or twice with little consequence if you quickly eliminate the distraction and if your message and behavior are strong. However, when you go on and on about your subject, oblivious to your body blocking the screen, you have upstaged both yourself and your support material. Worse yet, your slide information may be projected on your face and body, so the audience will be treating you like a slide! The result is sloppiness that is indelibly recorded in the audience's memory!

The antidote to poor visual aid management is to examine and try out the equipment before you use it and again, right before your presentation. This supports being prepared and in control. If possible, always test out your equipment in the room you will present in, before you start using it. Have a colleague sit in different locations in the room and give you feedback on visibility. If the audience can't see a slide, it is unlikely to be effective.

Pointing to a Slide

Related to standing in the light of the projector is pointing to a slide. This is because this gesture often crosses the light source, creating a shadow of your arm that hides what you intended to emphasize. There are several techniques to eliminate this distraction.

- Use your computer mouse and place the cursor on the information desired, or
- Use a laser pointer to point to the screen, careful to position yourself so only the red light beam highlights the detail in the slide;
- Use an old fashioned pedagogical pointer, a three-foot yardstick-like tool to point to the area of choice. Audiences won't snicker at the shadow *it* makes, but they will laugh at the shadow *you* make with your body.

Tracking and Tracing

Too often speakers forget they are holding these pointing tools. They no longer need them to identify as initially intended, but, still in hand, gesture with the tools making them gestural extensions. The audience, trying to follow the speaker's movement, is distracted by unconscious circling or other distracting movements.

When pointing to a slide, it is best to point and then release the pointing. When you point, you draw the audience's attention to what's on the screen. When you release the pointing, you signal your audience to listen to your words.

I can't emphasize enough the value of getting comfortable with these support tools ***before*** your presentation. You want a pulled-together presentation that showcases your expertise. Don't forfeit credibility because of clumsy handling of tools that are meant to help! Handle the tools before you practice the speech to get used to them. Then rehearse your presentation using the tools of choice.

Advancing a Slide too Soon or not Soon Enough

When you present using visual aids, you need to coordinate your illustrations with your story. Both seasoned and new presenters can find themselves ahead of, or behind their slides if they have not taken the time to practice this coordination. Even if you think you never miss when advancing your slides, it's a good idea to practice. Practice gives you an advantage. It gets you beyond the first time. Familiarity with material and equipment moves your mastery forward. This is true for musicians learning new compositions, athletes learning new plays, and speakers learning new techniques.

If you advance a slide too soon, it's better if you notice this before your audience does. As a presenter, you are also the **equipment manager** and the **audience**

observer. Usually your computer is close to you. What you see on your computer screen in front of you is exactly what is projected on the big screen behind you. You do not have to turn around to check if what is on the screen is correct. This should have been done once – right before the presentation, during your equipment check.

There may be a time where you do not realize you are either ahead or behind with a slide. If you are present with your audience, you will observe their facial expressions signaling that something is not right. This is an opportunity to pause, check in with the audience, or check your screen and make a necessary adjustment. You don't need any lengthy apology – a quick *I see I got ahead of myself* will do. Then review that information, observe the audience to confirm the confusion is cleared and move on to the next content area.

If someone else advances your slides for you, he/she must be intimately familiar with your presentation, your speaking style (pace and emphasis), and the equipment. The goal is a seamless coordination of visuals with speech. However, if you do become out of sync, it is perfectly okay to say: *Next slide please,* or *I think we want the slide before this one,* etc.

Talking Too Much while the Audience Processes the Slide

Polished speakers have learned to effectively coordinate their visual aids with their spoken messages. Many others, however, talk over the slide and do not allow sufficient time for the audience to process the information. By speaking, displaying visuals, and then pausing, the audience gets a moment of silence to process and reflect on the information. By *stopping* your talking, *you* get a moment to take in the audience's energy and attention, and to collect yourself for the next piece of information to be delivered.

Think of your speech as a multi-course feast. Each bit of information is a taste, a bite, a mouthful. Let your audience savor the information, and watch them swallow. Cleanse the palate with silence and serve the next course. Your listeners will neither feel stuffed and bloated, nor suffer from indigestion (data overload). Instead, your sensitivity to how the audience receives your information will make your presentation palatable and appreciated.

Letting the Slide Lead the Presentation Story

Most presenters use visuals in a very rote way. Click, there's the visual. *Now I look at the slide, read, explain it, click, go to the next slide.* They use visuals as cue cards or outlines. If the speaker's computer were to crash, he would be at a loss of words, unable to present.

Had the speaker developed his message or story and practiced it without visual aids, he would have been able to communicate without any visual support. If after creating the story, visual aids were inserted as illustrations, the computer crash would not have ruined the story, only eliminated the pictures.

Once the story is developed and organized, the need, type, and location of visual aids are determined. In this way, **the story leads and the visual aids reinforce.** You don't need a one-to-one ratio of ideas to visual aids. Visual aids need to be used sparingly. Your audience will anticipate a rote presentation if you routinely click and talk, click and talk, click and talk.

Be creative and conscious about your presentation support. Decide what information is best heard without visual display and what information is better understood with visual representation. As with storybooks, sometimes you see a picture, study it, and then read to find out more about it. Other times you start reading and a picture follows, depicting what you have just read.

You can lead with a visual or have a visual follow your spoken lead. You can speak without any visuals. You are the presenter. You choose. Exercise that choice and you will own your presentation and reflect your personal style.

Handouts as Visual Aids

A handout was once a piece of paper which highlighted key presentation points. It was often a bulleted summary, designed to reinforce the information the speaker presented. It was a "leave-behind," or "presentation takeaway" that reminded and reinforced what the listener had just heard.

Today handouts are used in different ways, and despite their prevalent use, many of these ways are ineffective. For example, a PowerPoint presentation is printed in thumbnail slide form and given to the audience at the start of the presentation. The audience, being human, splits their focus between the presenter's spoken words and the paper in their lap. They often read ahead as the speaker presents. Instead of having an audience whose attention is on the speaker, you have a splintered group of individuals doing its own thing.

In some meetings, the intention of this practice is for participants to be able to make notes per slide, and to recall the sequence of slides that created the presentation story. This practice of having the slides in front of the listener interferes with speaker influence but is an established practice for many scientific, teleconferenced, and global presentations.

Handouts can be distributed before, during, or after the speaker begins his presentation. My preference is that the speaker speaks without visuals for at least two to five minutes to establish his credibility and his ability to lead and tell his story. Then he can distribute handouts in silence. Distributing a handout after starting your presentation adds professional flair. Starting the presentation handing out paper and saying, perhaps, *"I'm handing out the presentation so you can follow along and take notes,"* is not wrong, but is kind of boring.

What to Do when Technology Fails

Have you ever attended a presentation where the presenter experienced technical difficulty right from the start? He asks for your patience and fiddles with this and that and as the seconds are ticking by, finally calls for tech support. The AV guru arrives five minutes later and takes another five to troubleshoot the problem. Sometimes it gets resolved, the presenter breathes a huge sigh of relief and the show goes on. Other times, the presenter is not so lucky. The screen remains blank and the presenter apologizing profusely, makes the most the time he has left.

For the first five to ten minutes, the audience hangs in with the speaker, understanding that things happen, and empathizes with the speaker's dilemma. But after ten minutes when it's clear the audio-visual plan is kaput, the audience gets edgy, annoyed or downright angry.

Electronic presentations can be tricky. They frequently cause a delay to your speaking start. When there is a problem, it affects both the speaker and listener.

Having a Presentation Plan B can be face-saving. You can have a flipchart or whiteboard in the room, or handouts. You can learn to tell your information in a way that gets people listening, rather than looking.

While plan B lacks in electronic flair, it gains in authentic communication. Make owning your message and being able to present it without slides, your presentation plan B.

VISUAL AID REVIEW

- Test and practice with equipment before you present
- Look at the audience, not at your slides
- Stand out of the light of the projector
- Point with a pointer; don't gesture with it
- Let the audience digest – watch them read or process. Stop talking.
- Plan when you want hand-outs distributed
- Have a visual aid Plan B

Part III
THE BEING STAGE

"Being must be felt. It can't be thought."
Eckhart Tolle

Chapter 19
BEING – Connection to Self

I was en route to a speech workshop a client had located online, one I had not heard about and that had piqued my curiosity. Being in a somewhat cocky mood, I questioned, "What can this speech trainer possibly know about presentation skills that I don't already know?" This thought kept hiccupping in my mind as I travelled from New Jersey to Virginia to check out this event. After all, I was a seasoned presentation coach with a twenty-year track record of speech coaching success. I had made a name for myself in local business circles, had been mentored by a brilliant trainer, and had invested much blood sweat and tears into my speech communications business.

Arriving at Union Station in Washington, DC, I took the Metro to a Virginia stop and then a $35 taxicab ride to the seminar location, and was surprised to be deposited in front of a home in a suburban development. I had expected a conference center or hotel or similar big business environment. Could I have the wrong address? I started to feel anxious, as I typically do when I am lost or in unfamiliar territory. I rang the doorbell and lightly knocked on the door.

I was graciously greeted by the homeowner who invited me into her kitchen for something to drink. I felt simultaneously awkward and interested as I informally met the workshop leader and participants. "OK," I said to myself, shedding my initial judgment, "this is, uh, different."

The seminar room was indeed the living room, with seating for twelve – some on the couch, some on easy chairs, and others on folding chairs. It hardly looked like a public speaking environment and didn't feel professional to me at all. After the leader introduced himself, his philosophy, and the program guidelines, we were ready to roll. "Finally," I thought, "teach me what I don't know, so I can go back to my business and use it to help others."

One by one, participants were called to speak – for only a measly two minutes! There were no creative openings, no developed storylines, no clever or memorable endings, just ordinary speaking. "You've got to be kidding" I heard my inner voice saying.

This is easy," I thought. But felt a knot in my gut as my name was called to be next. I must admit I was surprised by my body's response. I had never felt nervous speaking in public before. I got up from my seat and confidently stood before the living room group, practicing what I preach about posture and eye contact, and started to speak. And then, only seconds into my talk, I was abruptly yet gently told to stop, take a breath and look at one person at a time.

I was indignant! I knew my eye contact skills were well-honed and one of my speaking strengths. "I **am** looking at one person at a time," I said. I began again, and once more was told to stop and breathe, to take another breath, to "breathe again."

How dare he humiliate me like this! I know how to engage a group! Though embarrassed and angry, I acquiesced to the leader's direction. The silence stripped me naked and I sucked back tears of frustration. I felt chastised and criticized and wanted to leave – not just the room, but the area, the state, the universe. "Go home, go back on that train, back to your world," I told myself. "Return to what you do well." My anger intensified and I burst into tears. I was shocked, embarrassed, confused and exhausted.

And then the leader's red light turned green and I was allowed to speak. And I did – differently and from a place l of depth that I had not known I possessed.

Those thirty seconds of imposed silence were awkward and unnerving, yet they transformed my life and positively influenced my work. That was the impact of my first Speaking Circles™ a program for authentic and easy speaking.

Most presentation programs focus on two areas of competency: a clear, well-organized message and a personal delivery that eliminates distractions and packages the message well. These two areas are the ones I have addressed with my clients for over two decades, and they represent the thinking and doing components of the Speaking that Connects process.

However, there is another presentation component that can actually trump organization and platform skills, and that's what I call *Being*.

Being is probably the most powerful component of the Thinking, Doing, and Being process, and it has everything to do with audience attentiveness, audience buy-in, and speaker-audience connection. Though this component is neither your speech content nor your body language, it enhances both, because it has everything to do with *you* – the intimate, silent, aware self that you know best. This is the *You* that's neither thinking nor doing. It is the *You* that is simply *being*, perhaps the being part of "human being."

Being is energy, intention, trust, compassion, caring, confidence, and self-knowing. It's a state of awareness. It's your essence, your spirit, your inner nature, your soul-substance. And when it comes to speaking to groups, it's the juice of your presentation.

Without the *Being* aspect of ourselves, we would be thought and behavior machines. We regularly articulate facts and opinions and punctuate our words with our unique body communication. When we add *Being* to what we say and do, we align our thoughts and behaviors with our deepest nature. This alignment adds depth to our communications and resonates with that deeper place inherent in each and every individual in the audience.

Your audience is influenced by your message, your delivery, *and* your unique, non-ego Self, also known as *Being*, or essence. When you align your message and physical delivery with your true inner spirit, you create an unbelievable advantage. Your audience responds to this energy. They operate from thought, behavior, and spirit just as you do, and thus are more influenced by communication that integrates the three.

Think of it this way. Many people learn to play a specific instrument. They are familiar with composition, having learned and studied the notes. They have practiced so their fingers, breath and hands can execute those notes to perfection. But although different musicians are all playing the same composition with skills that support their best performance, there are individual nuances that make the music different. These nuances are unique to the individual, his nature and his *Being*. Another word for being is "presence." You might be surprised by the multiple dictionary definitions of this word:

a. the bearing, carriage, or *air* of a person;
b. the *quality* of poise and effectiveness that enables a performer to achieve a *close relationship* with his audience

c. something (*as a spirit*) felt or believed to be present,
d. the part or *space* within one's immediate vicinity.[2]

I have italicized these words to note the quality of silence and invisibility and the non-physical and non-vocal aspects of presence in these definitions.

While many people initially regard presence as physical appearance and talent or poise and effectiveness, upon deeper examination, they know that presence is something more than style and know-how. Though this "something more" is often difficult to put into words, your gut knows it is the quality that takes good to great, great to superb, and superb to out of this world!

In the western business world especially, talking about a quality as abstract and elusive as *Being* has been a no-no. Some training critics believe words like "spirit," "soul," and "presence" sound too religious, mystical or way-out. Smooth, effective and results-oriented has been the business orientation.

But guess what? Corporate clients are being referred to me because of their lack of executive *presence*, their need for enhanced *engagement*, and their desire to improve their *connection* with the audience. They have slick and often too-wordy PowerPoint slides, a lot of knowledge, and fairly good delivery, but they are missing the mojo.

Clients know the value of image, skill, and personality, yet intuitively sense that there is also something else: something non-verbal, non-physical, unique, and special that differentiates them from everyone else. They appreciate that **presence** is an essential part of

---

[2] Webster's New Collegiate Dictionary, A Merriam-Webster, G. & C. Merriam Company, Springfield, Massachusetts, 1980

presentation and has an effect on everything they do. They realize that connecting with one's own presence is the magic that allows connection to others.

To cultivate more awareness of presence, reflect on the exercises below.

Exercise:
Whom do you consider to have a strong presence and why?

_____

_____

How do you describe the difference between your favorite performers' (athlete, musician, actor, comic, dancer, etc) good and great performances?

_____

_____

_____

_____

To develop presence, you need to be open. You need to set aside judgment of yourself and others and to drop into your more intimate self, the self you reserve for a close friend. If you consider how you behave around a close friend, you realize that you are **more** yourself, that you operate from greater honesty, greater self-disclosure, greater *Being*. You allow your friend to see and know more of the total you, for better or for worse. You trust. You share. You allow yourself to be vulnerable and you connect, with or without words.

When you are silent and alone, you may realize and connect with your unique presence. Think of the contemplative or peaceful state of walking along a beach, resting in an easy chair, gazing at the stars, or melting into a baby's eyes. **No words, no thoughts, no doing.** This is what I mean by *being* and it is from this place that you want to overlay your ideas and body language to communicate effectively to a group.

The following exercise teaches "relational presence," a term used by Lee Glickstein, founder of Speaking Circles ™. In this exercise, the presence of one person meets the presence of another. On the surface, this exercise seems simple. However, the learning is often quite profound and always very individual. The medium of the connection is through the eyes.

The "Be With"[3] Exercise

In this exercise pairs of individuals face each other, usually seated about two feet apart. A facilitator asks you to "be with" the other person without talking, to gently be with the other person through soft, available eyes. A timer is set, and the participants are reminded to breathe and to **"receive"** the other person. There is no speaking, just the silent presence of the participants receiving one another eye-to-eye.

Having facilitated this process for several years, I am amazed by its simplicity and how it triggers so many different feelings in people. Inevitably, some dyads break

---

[3] Lee Glickstein, *Be Heard Now!* Broadway Books, NY 1998

the silence with tiny giggles or huge bursts of uncontrollable laughter. Some participants share concerns about staring and being rude, having interpreted receiving a soft, available gaze as a staring contest. Others confess that although they were not talking aloud, they were internally chatting up a storm: *What am I supposed to be seeing? Am I doing this right? Is he kidding? Okay, I'll look at just one eye. This is dumb. Oh, isn't that interesting, his eyes are asymmetrical? It would be interesting to draw her. What does this have to do with public speaking?*

This process is repeated for longer intervals and with different partners. Now here's what's particularly interesting. As participants become more practiced with this exercise, they become more comfortable sharing silence with each other. The mental chatter subsides, breathing becomes more natural, and many report a sense of peace, a renewed sense of personal calm, and a universal connection to community. Some say the exercise is relaxing and even comfortably intimate. Many share that they are more themselves and more comfortable in their own skin.

Although many speakers make strong and comfortable eye contact when they speak one-to-one, few seem comfortable when eye contact is made in silence. Eye contact in silence seems to push people's buttons. They initially cannot be comfortable with this connection without having something to say.

In the Doing section on body language, I talked about eye contact. This relational presence eye-to-eye exercise extends beyond looking and is deeper than the traditional eye contact previously discussed. This use of eyes penetrates *Being* and creates a more organic connection.

Consider eye contact as a fantastic painting with form, tone, and volume and relational-presence eye contact as an organic sculpture. The painting is two-dimensional and shows depth; the organic sculpture is a natural three-dimensional form.

When I first was introduced to this exercise as a participant, my reaction was initially analytical and visually-oriented. As an amateur artist, sitting across from my partner in silence, I examined the color and shape of my partner's eyes, the thickness of the eyelashes, the wrinkles and expression lines, and the overall facial symmetry. I was silent on the outside, but quite vocal on the inside, still active and still *doing*.

However, after being engaged in this exercise repeatedly, I felt my focus on physiognomy fade. Ultimately what happens is that the ego relaxes enough to take a back seat to the deeper presence of one's being. Being silent with another becomes just *being silent* with another – no judgment, no chatter, no monkey-mind, no artistic analysis.

This exercise is like a mini-course in meditation, but without the mantras and hours of sitting in stillness. In seconds for some, and in minutes for others, people connect with their inner selves in the presence of another. That's all there is to it. It's simple and enormously powerful.

Access to, and awareness of, your inner, non-physical and non-mental self is essential for audience engagement and connection. It's the ingredient that sustains audience interest, makes you memorable, and creates listening satisfaction. It's not the words or voice alone, nor your content, image, or excellent management of your body. It is the integration of your thinking and doing with your being that resonates with and sates your audience.

I'm reminded of an example I often use in training classes when I want to push the "presence" envelope. You have been allowed to board a plane early and you are comfortable in your own world, reading your magazine, or talking on your cell phone. Other passengers arrive and you take notice of them. An inner voice might say, *Oh, now there's an oversized person; I hope he doesn't sit next to me,* or *Look at the get up on her and that perfume is giving me a headache!* Or, *do you think that mother can put an end to that screaming kid?* Your human ego is at work again, thinking, judging, and separating your likes from your dislikes. It's a pretty common phenomenon.

It's almost time for take-off. Cell phones shut down. The oversized passenger buckles up in his bulkhead seat, the costumed and perfumed femme finishes cramming her extra baggage in the overhead, and the snot-dripping infant's cries are temporarily muted by a binky.

The plane takes off and is up in the air. Thinking everything is now as you like it, you settle in for a short snooze. Suddenly, the pilot interrupts your respite. He is on the loudspeaker announcing an emergency landing and requesting that everyone stay calm and quiet.

You're scared for your life!

The XXXL guy sitting in the bulkhead is now the one helping passengers with flotation devices and managing their safe exit. And while you certainly want safety for yourself, and *soon,* you hear your inner voice saying *Get the child off first.* And the over-scented woman with the overdone outfit turns out to be an emergency room technician who is initiating CPR to someone who has just fainted.

In a crisis such as this, the best in people shows up. People put prejudice aside, shed the superficial and operate from their authentic presence.

Speakers and audiences both are like the passengers on the plane. They come in all sizes and shapes and have all kinds of attitudes and opinions. We will never know everything about our audiences nor will our audiences know everything about us, the speakers, but we will have our presence and our human *being-ness* in common.

When a speaker risks being in the present moment and comfortable with silence, he allows himself to be authentically seen. **The audience connects not only with the speaker's presence, but also with his own.**

Now you have created a great and quiet common ground for what you have to say. From this place and "space," your audience is ready to listen to you at your best and mutual satisfaction is on its way.

Part IV
EXTERNALS, ENERGY & OTHER CONSIDERATIONS

"Energy is everywhere and in everything."
Anonymous

Chapter 20
Environment, Event, Equipment

Once I was asked to speak to a community group and was told that I would speak in one of the rooms at a church. I was prepared for a linoleum floor, stacking chairs, and windowless walls. To my surprise, the room I was given for my presentation was the chapel. Pews were the seating and behind me was Jesus Christ on a six foot crucifix. Had I taken the time to investigate the environment of my talk ahead of time, I would have requested another room. Having JC as my backdrop is strong competition, pews suggest piety and are not very comfortable and the whole tone of the atmosphere communicated religiousness and seriousness.

To make matters worse, the twenty people that came to my presentation chose to sit in the rear of the chapel, on both the right and left sides of a center aisle. In this holy environment, I felt awkward asking the "congregation" to find closer seats. Needless to say, this was not my favorite speaking experience!

Presenters are usually so concerned with what they say and how they say it that they often overlook opportunities that afford them a speaking advantage. The advantage I am referring to is familiarity with the speaking environment and its energy.

Your external environment influences both you and your audience, consciously and unconsciously. The size, shape, and color of the room, the furniture and its arrangement, the acoustics, exit signs, and room temperature are characteristics that can help or hurt your presentation.

For example, have you ever sat through a presentation in a room without air conditioning and the temperatures in the 90s? I have, and the unbearable heat can definitely compromise the attention of even the most interested audience.

Speaking from a stage is another environment that challenges many speakers who may otherwise be comfortable in the more traditional settings of conference or training rooms. If you've never had the experience of being on stage, you may very well feel awkward and even overwhelmed by its spaciousness. Suddenly you are *too* aware of your walk. Each step you take feels oddly different and less natural than usual. The standing still that usually feels just right in the meeting room now feels overly rigid. You may become self-conscious, or feel small, perhaps feeling unworthy or unempowered. Yes, environment can affect your comfort zone and play havoc with your confidence and performance.

For example, have you ever spoken in a too crowded room where the attendees were squished like sardines? I was once the speaker at an annual event where the audience had been used to a cushy luncheon environment. However, the year that I spoke, the event logistics changed at the last hour. A more prestigious client was given the elegant room and my audience found themselves in a cinder block student center sitting on metal folding chairs at long cafeteria tables, rather than on padded dining room armchairs at linen-covered round tables.

My talk was received well, but I had to work harder than usual to satisfy the audience. Their disappointment and discomfort challenged their listening and made engaging and connecting with them much more difficult. They had to work at letting go of their disappointment about their environment to receive me openly and focus their listening. I could feel their frustration as well as their effort to manage and overcome it, both energies competing with their desire to be fully present to the speaker. The bottom line is that environments have their own energies and essences, just as do speakers and audiences. Do whatever you can to improve the environment for yourself and your audience and definitely, eye-ball the room in advance so you are as prepared as you can be!

Room Arrangement

Similarly, the arrangement of a room has its own energy, which influences you as a speaker. Presenters often find themselves speaking at a dinner, lunch, or breakfast meeting. The room arrangement can involve round tables that accommodate six to ten people. Because many of the audience have their backs and sides to the speaker, the speaker is often compelled to wander through the room in order to engage and feel closer to the crowd. However, sometimes, there's insufficient room to move, let alone meander, and you find yourself standing at a podium with a microphone speaking to the backs of half the audience.

Seating styles will influence speaker and audience, too. Some seating arrangements will be theater style without any aisles; others will have left and right seating with a central aisle and still others may have three sections of seating: right, left, and center. How deep the rows are will affect a speaker's ability to connect with the audience, especially those at the back of the room. If the environment is arranged in classroom style, the speaker has to deal with table-top boundaries and pedagogical perceptions. Nobody wants to feel as if he's in high school again. There is often the tendency for the listeners to write or doodle, just because there is a surface in front of them, a surface that reminds them of school.

One company decided to have its town hall meetings "in the round." The speaker would be on a slightly raised platform with the audience in concentric circles around him. The idea was to minimize hierarchical boundaries. With this design, senior staff would not be in the first six rows for example, but instead, in the first circular tier.

This is a great idea in theory, but few speakers have ever had any practice or direction in speaking in the round. It's uncomfortable not knowing how and when to turn and hard to be present to the whole room when you can't see the people and realize half of your audience is watching you from the rear. If an organization is intent on the creative, I'm all for it. Just give the speakers some coaching and an opportunity to practice beforehand. A speaker's comfort affects his presentation, the audience and the overall success of an event.

While you will not be able to control every presentation venue, eye-balling your environment a day or more before your presentation alerts you to potential challenges. Knowing what you'll be dealing with ahead of the event, gives you the opportunity to request or make some modifications. This knowledge allows you to compensate for environmental structures or make a shift in presentation style. Being aware of your speaking environment, even if it is less than desirable, is also one unknown you now know about. With less environmental surprises, you have a greater degree of comfort and control. **An experienced presenter will adapt his style to his audience and environment as needed. A smart presenter will view his speaking environment before his presentation.**

The Speaking Event

In addition to learning about your presentation environment, you will want to reflect on the actual speaking event. What type of event is it? Is it a dinner meeting, convention, competition, wedding?

At what time of day will you speak? Will you be speaking during a meal? If so, will your speech follow or precede the food or will your speaking compete with the audience's eating?

I recently watched a speaker present while the crowd wolfed down dinner. How comfortable would it be for you to observe your audience gorge while you engage them with food for thought?

Do you know if you are the only speaker on the agenda or one of many speakers? Do you know who or what precedes or follows your presentation? How much time is slated for each speaker? What is your plan if the speaker before you exceeds his allotted time? Are you prepared to condense your speech from a planned forty minutes to an unplanned seven?

The situations reflected by these questions are commonplace. Presenters who contemplate these potential challenges will definitely be more Murphy's Law- prepared and this preparation can prove a presentation plus.

Recently one of my clients hosted a scientific congress. She had spent three months planning the event, securing speakers, motivating employees to attend, reserving the rooms, publicizing the event, creating the ambiance, and rehearsing her presentation. The opening address was to be delivered by the most senior professional of the organization and his presentation was impeccably prepared by the company's internal communications department. However, on the day of the event, instead of sticking with the agenda, this Vice President decided to speak a *little* extemporaneously before delivering the PowerPoint presentation prepared on his behalf.

His "little bit" took forty-five minutes instead of fifteen, which caused the relaxed networking lunch to be both shortened and short-changed. The afternoon speakers scrambled to reduce their presentations by half. Many of the speakers ended their presentation in the middle while others uncomfortably apologized to the audience as they skipped over slides and scrambled to get to their conclusion and next steps.

This unfortunately happens more times than not. Unless you are the first speaker of day or the first in the afternoon session, you run the risk of having your time taken away by a preceding speaker with poor presentation time management.

Speakers must be prepared to reduce their allotted time in half, in thirds and to sound bites. When you are a presenter in a series of presentations, be prepared with a presentation back-up plan. Know how to reduce your presentation from forty-five minutes to twenty, from twenty to five and from five to two.

My client, the conference emcee, abandoned her planned presentation, articulated her bottom-line message, introduced the next speaker and made up the time. She saw an opportunity, seized it, and saved the conference from going on too long, something audiences rarely appreciate.

Equipment: Microphones, Podiums and Teleprompters

Microphones are generally helpful when the speaker is before crowds of fifty or more. However, room size, room acoustics, and the speaker's own vocal ability to project loudly enough for the audience to hear, are drivers that determine whether a microphone is worth using.

Some microphones are part of a podium or lectern. Microphones with cords allow you to move about. Of course, cord length will determine your range of movement, but you can get extension cables for these microphones if you need or want more room to roam.

Lavaliere microphones are designed to be worn on your lapel and can be corded or cordless. Whether wired or wireless, hand held or collar–attached, the microphone is an energy-boosting tool designed to amplify your voice. With regard to microphone management there are several concerns to consider.

Since amplification changes how you sound to yourself, it's always a good idea to practice at least a small portion of your speech with a microphone so you can get used to hearing your amplified voice. Hearing one's amplified voice for the first time can make some speakers feel uneasy and this uneasiness at the start of the presentation can set the wrong tone, compromising overall effectiveness.

On the other hand, some presenters can become too relaxed when they use microphones. Because they are now easily heard, they may speak with less passion and enthusiasm, unconsciously minimizing their energy and the vocal impact on the audience.

Presenters with limited microphone experience can also create shrill and invasive electronic feedback from high-volume settings. Their "testing, one, two, three" or a "blowing into the microphone to see if it is working routine" are true signs of an amateur as well as an auditory affront to the audience.

Another no-no is forgetting to turn off the power on the power supply for a lavaliere microphone. Trade secrets and bathroom banter are well-documented negative outcomes when microphones have remained in the "on" position long after the presentation has ended.

If you wear chains or pearls, you want to be sure the movement of your jewelry doesn't knock into the microphone as you gesture and move, causing the amplified *clonk* that interrupts both your speaking and your audience's listening. And if you have snaked the power pack cord beneath your jacket with the pack on your belt, please be certain you are buttoned correctly when you get up to the stage. Nothing is more embarrassing than seeing a seasoned professional who is all askew as a result of buttoning a top button into a middle buttonhole. No matter how astute the speaker, the audience just can't get beyond the mishap. They feel embarrassed for the speaker and spend the whole time wondering how they can help him, at the expense of listening to what he has to say.

If you're using a microphone, make time for some pre-presentation microphone practice. A microphone presents one more presentation element to manage. When it's time for you to speak, you want the bulk of your energy and attention on your message and audience, not on your amplification equipment.

Podiums

A podium or lectern is an apparatus that encases a speaker on three sides, provides a surface for the speaker's notes or laptop, and is usually equipped with a microphone. Some modern lecterns have electronic controls for the room's other audio-visual equipment built into them. There are buttons to raise and lower the podium, switches that raise and lower the projection screen, dials to increase the volume of the microphone, and knobs to dim the lights in the room. The construction of a podium or lectern is usually wood or particle-board. Podiums are typically located at the front of a room in the right or left corner.

Podiums project formality. They are generally used by CEOs for town hall meetings, by presidents for State of the Union addresses, and politicians for city government sessions. Podiums are also part of the formality of large conferences during which speakers present from stage. That said, schools, churches, universities, hotels and conference centers generally own at least one podium.

Whether you choose to use a podium or not should be a matter of taste and choice. However, sometimes speakers choose to speak at a podium to mask their nervousness or to camouflage their physique.

Here are some podium facts to ponder when deciding to speak from a podium.

- Because of their composition, podiums absorb sound. You will have to speak significantly louder if the lectern does not have a microphone.

- Most lecterns are boxy in design. A short person will appear like a child behind one. Standing on a concealed footstool will add the height necessary to create a balance between the person and the lectern.

- A narrow lectern looks more like a bookstand and will exaggerate the girth of a large person. Checking out the room ahead of time will allow you to determine if a particular piece of equipment serves you or not.

- With a lectern you work harder to make a connection with your audience because a lectern energetically and physically creates a boundary between speaker and listeners.

If you do decide to speak from behind a podium, there are several *doing* best practices to keep in mind.

- Standing still to start is even more important when behind a podium than standing still without a lectern. Because of the perpendicular structure of a podium, ambient movement is magnified and can become a distraction to the audience.

- Keep your hands lightly on the ledge of the podium top and available for gesturing. If your hands are in neutral at your sides, you will probably not gesture, or if you do, you might bang them against the structure in your attempt to use them naturally.

- Because there is a platform or table-top for notes and papers, there is a tendency to use notes and papers. Rummaging through and rustling papers is distracting to your audience and detracts from your credibility. If you need to rely on written notes, write them on heavier paper such as cardstock to reduce the paper-rustling sound.

Teleprompters

A teleprompter is a device that displays the text or script of a speech. It is used in formal speaking settings such as presidential addresses, professional conferences, and special event programs; speaking that is often on a stage. Modern teleprompters interface with computers so that scrolling text is projected onto clear screens for the speaker to read. You can set the pace of the scroll to match a speaker's natural speaking cadence. Basically, a teleprompter replaces written notes and allows the speaker to look outward rather than downward, appearing as if he or she is speaking spontaneously or has committed the speech to memory.

Some teleprompter equipment forces the speaker to look downwards, not at podium notes, but at the level of the floor. "Doghouses" are boxes that house the scrolling script. They are often preferred to clear pole-like teleprompters because they are less obvious and less intrusive to the audience. In either case, the speaker reads a scrolling script on two or more of these apparatuses.

Few people use teleprompters with ease. Even Barack Obama who is considered a very polished speaker, has been criticized for looking too obviously "left and right" as he reads his speech.

If you have the occasion to speak with a teleprompter, be certain to rehearse your presentation more than once, to acclimate yourself to the equipment and to ensure your teleprompter technician is in sync with your speaking style.

Most presenters I've worked with wish they could practice with a teleprompter before they actually have to work with one. However, because of the cost of this equipment, few companies and coaches actually own them. Speakers get to rehearse with them at the pre-event rehearsal, most often the night before the presentation event.

Another option is CuePrompter, an online teleprompter, http://www.cueprompter.com. You enter your speech text, indicate how fast you want the prompter to run and the text is then displayed on your computer screen, which allows you to get used to the scrolling text in the comfort of your own home or office.

Chapter 21
Rehearsal and Practice

I don't believe that practice makes perfect, but I do believe that practice makes improved. I'm also not an advocate of *more is better.* Too much practice can be detrimental to your speech.

The key reason for rehearsing your speech is so you that you hear and feel your speech before your audience hears it. Speaking aloud transforms thought into voice which brings the speech outside the speaker's body. The speaker can now become his own listener. This is the real value of rehearsal.

My compromise for those who say they become frustrated and fizzle out when they practice without an audience is this: rehearse the opening and the closing of your presentation at least one time. This is what audiences remember most, what you say to start and what you say to finish. Having a smooth take-off and a smooth landing will give you control, confidence and comfort.

Speaking to a few friends, colleagues or family is better than speaking to walls, mirrors, and cameras. However, if no one is available, standing and saying your opening and closing aloud in a room of chairs will move your speaking development forward.

Practice your non-verbal behaviors as well as your verbal content. Walk and breathe, position yourself, and anchor your feet. Scan your body for nervous energy. Bathe the nervous areas with breath, keeping your thoughts silent. Look at someone's eyes and smile. Look at another pair of eyes as you feel and scan your breath. Greet your audience and speak your opening aloud, one pair of eyes at a time.

Using the format tool in Chapter 5, mention the three content areas of your presentation and then go straight to the conclusion. Breathe, look at someone, talk, share with another, talk, share again and then end.

Pause after your last words. *Really* pause. Say to yourself *"the end, one, two, three, four."* Allow this spaciousness, these few seconds of time, to signal the end of your prepared presentation. Then following that spaciousness, thank your audience, step forward, and invite your audience to participate by asking for their questions.

This is my brand of rehearsal and I hope it serves you well.

Chapter 22
Final Remarks

Ten steps to prepare a targeted message, five body elements for managing nervousness and distraction and one conscious intention to connect with your inner self, your material and your audience. Although these ideas are presented as separate entities, they are really very much intertwined.

When you have a clear plan, you own and control your information. This frees up mental energy which allows you to be more physically present. Energizing your body, as with grounding and breathing, connects your physical self with your inner self. Connecting with your inner self helps you integrate your information in a way that resonates with and influences your listeners.

This process works and many readers will reap rewards from reading alone. However, for those who want a more hands-on experience, I recommend a ***Speaking that Connects*™** workshop or individual coaching. These programs will refine your technique, provide opportunities to practice and further grow your confidence and presence. For specific questions or needs, please feel free to write me at Sinett@speakingthatconnects.com.

In closing, may you fully enjoy the presentation process as you present with confidence and engage your audience.

Eileen N. Sinett

Acknowledgements

This book would not have been written had I not had the support of my friends, family and colleagues.

In particular, I want to thank Ed Tseng, Peak Performance trainer, speaker and author, who held me accountable for writing my first draft. Had I defaulted on this agreement, I would have been sending him and his wife to Europe and picking up the tab for travel and dinner at their favorite Parisian restaurant.

Thank you Karen Hodges Miller, publisher, editor and writing coach, for keeping me on track and bringing this book to completion. Thank you for helping me hear my written voice.

HUGE gratitude to Barbara Stange, my administrative goddess extraordinaire, whose flexibility, optimism and creative vision she so generously shared. From title to cover to content, she was present with me all the way.

For their exceptional editing expertise I thank Scott Morgan, Sharon Sheiman, Karen Hodges Miller, Marilynn Winston and Barbara Stange.

The title and the cover of this book seem to have had nine lives! For input and insight on the final title, I thank Loraine Kulick, Sharon Sheiman, Jeanne Murphy, Paul Schindel, Karen Hodges Miller, Ellen Tozzi, Ed Tseng, Lynda Klau, Martin R. Schached and Tracey Haneman.

For the cover design I am extremely grateful for the team collaboration of David Haneman, Barbara Stange, Karen Hodges Miller and Tracey Haneman. Thank you David and Barbara for the long hours invested in designs that were "almosts;" and thank you Tracey for your Photoshop finesse and font flair.

Finally, I want to thank some of the professionals who mentored, influenced and/or supported my work: Thom Runyon, Joe Kowalski, Bill Dorman, Kathy Shipman, Marian Thier, Patricia Encinas, Ather Williams, Jr., Tom Kereszti, Francis J. Nead, Lynn Kroeger, Sherri Waryasz, Bill Tortoriello, Jim Cyr, Jay Lawton, Joanne Pfleiderer, Liz Meyers Bertty, Jeannette Thannikary, Lee Glickstein, Doreen Hamilton, Beth Way, Cliff Harwin, Sam Russell, Diana Barbu, Kristen Vockel, Sarah McLoughlin Tseng, Rob Gough, Barbara F. Fox, Sreehari Gopal, Noelle Stary, Ellen Tozzi, Jack Becher and all my Speaking that Connects business breakfast buddies.

Last but not least, for their love and support that goes well beyond the writing of this book, I thank my parents, my six siblings, my daughter and my long-term best friends (you know who you are).

Thank you all.

APPENDIX

Some of My Favorite Resources

Bolton, Robert, **People Skills,** Simon & Schuster, NY, 1979

Craig, Malcolm, **Thinking Visually,** Continuum, 2000

Decker, Bert, **You've Got to Be Believed to Be Heard**, St. Martin's Press, NY, 1991

Duarte, Nancy, **Slide:ology: The Art and Science of Great Presentations**, 2008

Duarte, Nancy, **Resonate: Present Visual Stories that Transform Audiences,** 2009

Fletcher, Leon, **How to Speak Like a Pro,** Ballantine Books, NY, 1983

Glickstein, Lee, **Be Heard Now!** Broadway Books, NY 1998

Hamilton, Doreen, Ph.D., **Essential Speaking: The 7-Step Guide to Finding Your Real Voice,** 2009

Hendricks, William, M. Holliday, R. Mobley, K. Stienbrecher**,** *Secrets* **of Power Presentations,** Career Press, Franklin Lakes, NJ, 1996

Hoff, Hoff**,** *I Can See You Naked,* Andrews & McMeel, a Universal Press Syndicate Company, Kansas City, Missouri, 1992

Hoff, Ron, **Do Not Go Naked Into Your Next Presentation,** Andrews & McMeel, Kansas City, 1997

Klepper, Michael M. with Robert Gunther, **I'd Rather Die Than Give a Speech,** Carol Publishing Group, Citadel Press, 1994

Lambert, Clark, **The Business Presentations Workbook,** Prentice-Hall, NJ, 1998

Larsen, Gail, **Transformational Speaking,** IUnivervse, Inc, 2007
Carole M. Mablekos, Ph.D., **Presentations That Work,** Institute of Electrical & Electronic Engineers, Inc., New York, 1938

Mandel, Steve, **Effective Presentation Skills,** Crisp Publications, Inc. Menlo Park, California, 1987

Millman, Dan, **The Peaceful Warrior's Path to Everyday Enlightenment, (CD set)** Nightingale-Conant Corp., 2008

Morrisey, G. L. and T. L. Sechrest, **Effective Business and Technical Presentations,** Addison-Wesley Publications, Reading, Mass. 1987

Nirenberg, Jesse S., Ph.D., **Getting Through to People,** Prentice-Hall, Englewood Cliffs, NJ, 1963

Peoples, David A., **Presentations Plus,** John Wiley & Sons, New York, 1988

Peoples, David A., **Selling to the Top,** John Wiley & Sons, New York, 1988

Reynolds, Garr, **Presentation Zen, Simple Ideas on Presentation Design and Delivery,** New Riders, 2008

Reynolds, Garr, **Presentation Zen – The Video,** New Riders, 2009

Scharmer, C. Otto, **Theory U, Leading from the Future as It Emerges,** The Society for Organizational Learning, Inc, 2007

Senge, Peter, C. Otto Scharmer, Joseph Jaworski and Betty Sue Flowers, **Presence,** Doubleday, 2004

Skopec, Eric W., **Business and Professional Speaking**, Prentice-Hall, Englewood Cliffs, NJ, 1983

Tolle, Ekhart, **A New Earth: Awakening to Your Life's Purpose,** First Plume Printing, 2005

Tolle, Ekhart, **The Power of NOW,** New World Library, 1999

Toogood, Granville N., **The Articulate Executive,** McGraw Hill, New York, NY 1996

Weissman, Jerry J., **Presenting to Win: The Art of Telling Your Story,** 2008

Wydro, Kenneth, **Think On Your Feet**, Prentice-Hall, Englewood Cliffs, NJ, 1981

www.Ted.com
www.Cueprompter.com

Speaking that Connects: Training

Speaking that Connects™ is a presentation program that develops presenter clarity, confidence and connection. It is a step by step process that involves thinking, doing and being exercises to enhance personal and professional growth. Program modules address:

- Nervousness and anxiety
- Message Development
- Presentation Organization
- Body Language Practices
- Voice Projection
- Personal Presence
- Visual Aid Design and Management
- The Question and Answer Period

Speaking that Connects ™ is available as a public workshop in multiple formats. This can include a pre-workshop one-one coaching session and ReHearsals, a follow-up program for continuous practice and just in time presentation support. Speaking that Connects ™ can be customized for your business or organization.

Sinett@speakingthatconnects.com
www.speakingthatconnects.com

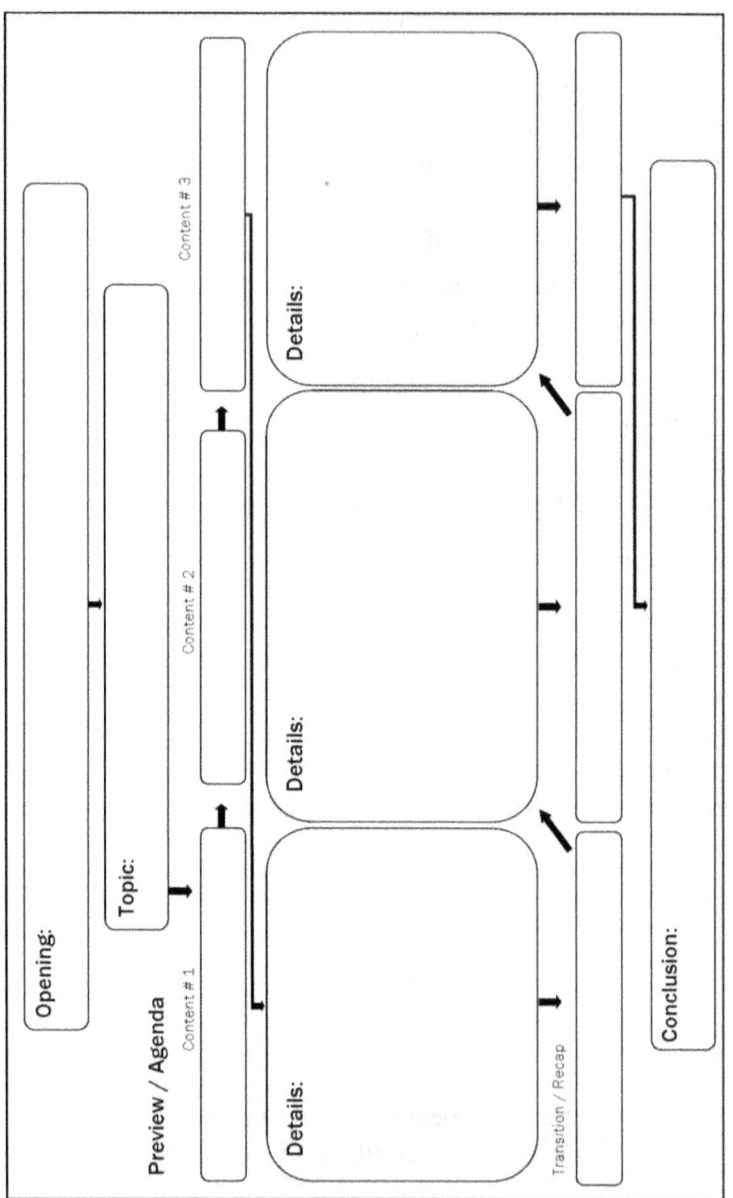

Figure 5.1 Format Worksheet

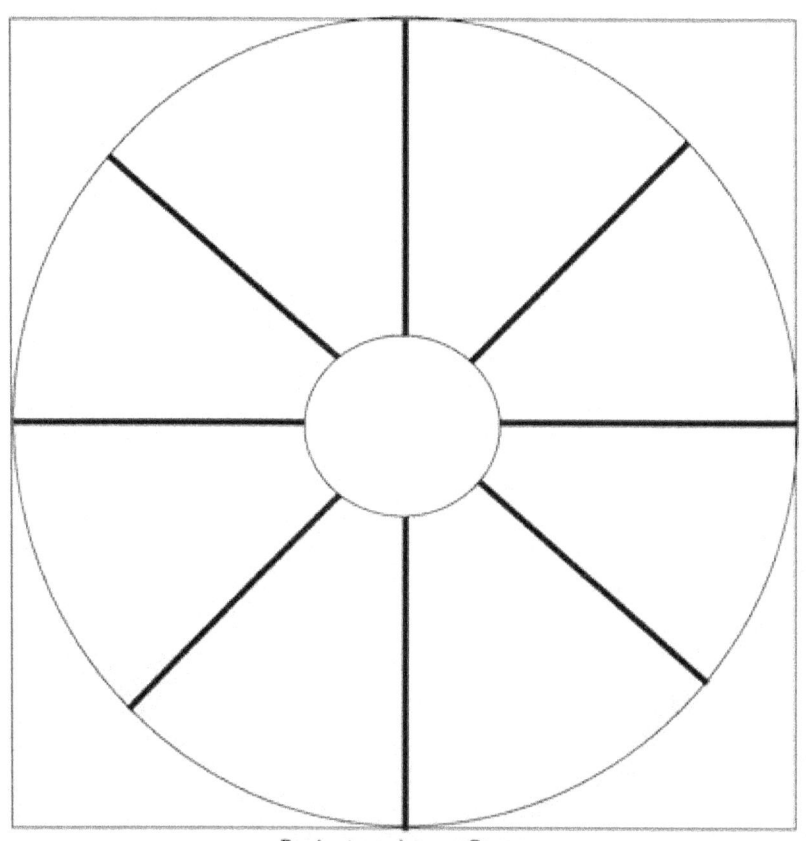
Brainstorming on Paper

www.ingramcontent.com/pod-product-compliance
Lightning Source LLC
Chambersburg PA
CBHW071434160426
43195CB00013B/1898